SOLDIER C: SAS

SECRET WAR IN ARABIA

80p

SOLDIER C: SAS

SECRET WAR IN ARABIA

Shaun Clarke

First published in Great Britain 1993
22 Books, Invicta House, Sir Thomas Longley Road,
Rochester, Kent

Copyright © 1993 by 22 Books

The moral right of the author has been asserted

A CIP catalogue record for this book is available from the
British Library

ISBN 1 898125 05 8

10 9 8 7 6 5 4 3 2 1

Typeset by Hewer Text Composition Services, Edinburgh
Printed and bound in Great Britain by
Caledonian International Book Manufacturing Ltd, Glasgow

PRELUDE

Framed by the veils of his Arab *shemagh*, the guerrilla's face was good-humoured, even kindly. This made it all the more shocking when he expertly jabbed his thin-bladed knife through Sa'id's eyelid and over the top of his eyeball, twisting it downward to slice through the optic nerve at the back of the retina and gouge the eye from its socket.

The old man's pain was indescribable, exploding throughout his whole being, drawing from him a scream not recognizably human and making him shudder and strain frantically against his tight bonds. Glancing down through the film of tears in his remaining eye, he saw his own eyeball staring up at him from the small pool of blood in the guerrilla's hand.

'Will you now renounce your faith?' the guerrilla asked. 'What say you, old man?'

Racked with pain and disbelief, his heart racing too quickly, Sa'id glanced automatically across the clearing. He saw the troops of the Sultan's Armed Forces lying on the ground, shot dead with pistols, soaked in blood. Directly above them, the bodies of other village elders were dangling lifeless from ropes.

Beyond the hanged men, clouds of smoke were still rising from the smouldering ashes of homes put to the torch. The sounds of wailing women, screaming girls and pleading men rose above sporadic outbursts of gunfire and hoarse, self-satisfied male laughter.

Life in this and the other villages of the country had become nightmarish in recent months, but today, in this particular village, all hell had broken loose.

First, at dawn, the Sultan's troops had encircled the village to accuse the people of aiding the guerrillas and to prevent them doing so in the future. This they did by torching the whole settlement, cementing over the well without which the villagers could not survive, and hanging a few suspected communist sympathizers from ropes tied to poles hammered hastily into the ground. Then, in the late afternoon, the communist guerrillas had arrived to terrorize the already suffering Muslim villagers and, in particular, to pursue their merciless campaign of making the repected elders of each community renounce their faith.

'So, old man,' the guerrilla taunted Sa'id, still holding the bloody eyeball in his hand for him to see, 'will you renounce your vile Muslim faith or do I gouge out the other one?'

Still in a state of shock, barely aware of his own actions, Sa'id nevertheless managed to croak, 'No, I cannot do that. No matter what you do to me, I cannot renounce my faith.'

'You're a stubborn old goat,' the guerrilla said. 'Perhaps, if you don't care for yourself, you'll be more concerned for your daughters.' Casually throwing Sa'id's eyeball into the dirt, he turned to the armed guerrillas behind him. 'Take the Muslim bitches,' he said, 'and make proper whores of them.'

'No!' Sa'id cried out in despair, as the men raced into the ruins of his half-burnt home and the screams of his virgin daughters rent the air. It went on a long time: the girls screaming, the guerrillas laughing, while Sa'id sobbed, strained against his bonds, tasted the blood still pouring from his eye socket, and mercifully slipped in and out of consciousness.

But he was still coherent when his three adolescent daughters, their clothes bloody and hanging in shreds from their bruised, deflowered bodies, were thrown out of the ruins of his mud-and-thatch hut to huddle together, sobbing shamefully, in the dust.

Even as the horrified Sa'id stared at them with his one remaining eye, the guerrilla with the good-humoured face turned to him and asked, '*Now* will you renounce your faith, old man?'

When Sa'id, too shocked to respond, simply stared blankly out of his good eye, the guerrilla snorted with disgust, gouged out his other eye, slashed through his bonds even as the old man was screaming, and stepped aside to let him fall to the ground.

Sa'id could hear his daughters wailing, even though he could not see them. Nor could he see the other raped and beaten women, the men dangling from ropes, the shot SAF troops, the burned ruins of the village huts and the life-giving well sealed with cement. All he saw was the darkness in which he would spend the rest of his days.

Sa'id wept tears of blood.

1

'Badged!' Trooper Phil Ricketts said, proudly holding up his beige beret to re-examine the SAS winged-dagger badge stitched to it the previous day by his wife, Maggie. 'I can hardly believe it.'

'Believe it, you bleedin' probationer,' said Trooper 'Gumboot' Gillis, who was wearing his own brand-new badged beret. 'You earned it, mate. We *all* did!'

'I'm surprised I actually made it,' said Andrew Winston, a huge black Barbadian, glancing around the crowded Paludrine Club and clearly proud to be allowed into it at last, 'particularly as I almost gave up once or twice.'

'We probably all thought about it,' said Tom Purvis, 'but that's all we did. Otherwise we wouldn't be drinking in here.' He glanced around the noisy, smoky recreation room of 22 SAS Regiment. 'We're here because, although we may have thought about it, we didn't actually give up.'

'I thought about it once,' Ricketts said. 'I'll have to admit that. Once – only once.'

He had done so during that final, awful night on the summit of Pen-y-fan. At other times during the 26 weeks of relentless physical and mental testing, he had wondered what he was doing there and if it was all worth it. But only that once had the thought of actually giving up crossed his mind – in the middle of that dark, stormy night in the Brecon Beacons, where, for one brief, despairing moment, he thought he had reached the end of his tether.

Even now, he could only look back on the rigours of Initial Selection, 'Sickeners One and Two', Continuation Training, Combat Training and, finally, the parachute course, with a feeling of disbelief that he had actually undergone it and lived to tell the tale. He had arrived at the SAS camp of Bradbury Lines, in the Hereford suburb of Redhill, in the full expectation that he was in for a rough time, but nothing had quite prepared him for just how rough it actually turned out to be.

'What you are about to undergo,' the Squadron Commander, Major Greenaway, had informed over a hundred recruits that first morning as they sat before him on rows of hard seats in the training wing theatre, or Blue Room, of Bradbury Lines, 'is the most rigorous form of testing ever devised for healthy men. No matter how good you believe yourselves to be as soldiers – and if you didn't think you were good, you wouldn't be here now – you will find yourselves tested to the very limits of your endurance. Our selection process offers no mercy. You can fail at any point over the 26 weeks. Some will fail on the first day, some on the very last. If you are failed, you will find yourselves standing on Platform Four of Redhill Station, being RTU'd.' A few of the listening men glanced at each other, but no one dared say a word. 'There is no appeal,' Greenaway continued. 'Only a small number of you will manage to complete the course successfully – a *very* small number. Let that simple, brutal truth be your bible from this moment on.'

It was indeed a brutal truth, as Ricketts was to discover from the moment the briefing ended and the men were rushed from the Blue Room – passing under a sign reading 'For many are called but few are chosen' – to the Quartermaster's stores to be kitted out with a bergen backpack, sleeping bag, webbed belts, a wet-weather poncho, water bottles, a heavy prismatic compass, a brew kit, three 24-hour ration packs and Ordnance Survey maps of the Brecon Beacons and Elan Valley, where the first three-day trial, known as Sickener One, would take place.

Once kitted out, they hurried from the QM's stores to the armoury, where they were supplied with primitive Lee Enfield 303 rifles. Allocated their beds, or 'bashas', in the barracks of the training wing, they were allowed to drop their kit off in the 'spider' – an eight-legged dormitory area – and have a good lunch in the cookhouse. Immediately after that, the harsh selection process began.

'Christ,' Gumboot said, placing his pint glass on the table and licking his wet lips, 'it seems a lot longer than it was. Only six months! It seems like six years.'

Ricketts remembered it only too well. The few days leading up to Sickener One were filled with rigorous weapons training and arduous runs, fully kitted, across the deceptively gentle hills of the Herefordshire countryside, each one longer and tougher than the one before, and all of them leading to a final slog up an ever-steeper gradient that tortured lungs and muscles.

The first of the crap-hats, or failures, were weeded out during those runs and humiliatingly RTU'd, or returned to their original unit. Those remaining, now fully aware of just how many failures there would be, instinctively drew into themselves, not wanting to become too friendly with those likely to soon suffer the same fate.

'And to think,' Tom Purvis said, shaking his

head from side to side in wonder, 'that at the time we thought nothing could be worse than Sickener One!'

'It's helpful not to know too much,' Jock McGregor said.

'It sure is, man,' big Andrew added, flashing his perfect teeth. 'If we'd known that Sickener One was just kids' stuff compared to what was coming, we'd never have stuck it out for the rest.'

It was a greatly reduced number of SAS aspirants from various British Army regiments who had awakened in the early hours of a Saturday morning, showered, shaved, pulled on their olive-green uniforms, or OGs, picked up their rifles and dauntingly heavy bergens, then hurried out to the waiting four-ton Bedford trucks. After being driven north along the A470, they were eventually dropped off in the Elan Valley, in the Cambrian Mountains of mid-Wales. An area of murderously steep hills and towering ridges, it had been chosen for its difficult, dangerous terrain and harsh weather as the perfect testing ground for Sickener One. This gruelling three-day endurance test is based on hiking and climbing while humping a heavily packed bergen and weapons, then repeatedly 'cross-graining the bukits'.

Derived from the Malay – Malaysia was

where the exercise was first practised – this last expression means going from one summit or trig point to another by hiking up and down the steep, sometimes sheer hills rather than taking the easy route around them. It takes place in the most rugged terrain and the foulest weather imaginable, including fierce wind, rain or blinding fog. Each conquered summit is followed by another, and the slightest sign of reluctance on the part of the climber is met by a shower of abuse from a member of the directing staff (DS), or – a psychological killer – by the softly spoken suggestion that the candidate might find it more sensible to give up and return to the waiting Bedfords.

Those taking this advice seriously were instantly failed and placed on RTU, never to be given the chance to try again. This happened to many during the three days of Sickener One.

Those who survived the first day, even though exhausted and disorientated, then had to basha down at the most recent RV, or rendezvous, no matter how hostile the terrain. Invariably, when they did so, they were frozen and wet, often with swollen feet and shoulders blistered by the bergen. They were then forced to spend the night in the same appalling weather, eating 24-hour rations heated on portable hexamine stoves, drinking tea boiled on the same, before bedding down in sleeping bags protected from the elements only by waterproof ponchos.

Given the filthy, windy weather – for which that time of the year had been deliberately chosen – few of the men got much sleep and the next day, even wearier than before, they not only cross-grained more bukits, but were faced with the dreaded entrail ditch, filled with stagnant water and rotting sheep's innards, standing in for the blood and bone of butchered humans. The candidates had to crawl through this vile mess on their bellies, face down, holding their rifles horizontally – it was known as the 'leopard crawl' – ignoring the stench, trying not to swallow any of the mess, though certainly swallowing their own bile when they brought it up. Failure to get through the entrail ditch was an RTU offence which further reduced the number of aspirants.

'I fucking dreaded that,' Tom said, lighting a cigarette and puffing smoke. 'It was only the thought of Platform Four that kept me going when things got rough.'

'Right,' said Bill Raglan, who was born and bred in Pensett, in the West Midlands, and had little education but a lot of intelligence. Bill's face was badly scarred from the many fights he had been in before the regular Army channelled his excess energy in a more positive direction. 'Can you imagine the humiliation, standing there with the other rejects? Then having to go back to your old regiment with your tail between your legs. That kept *me* going all right!'

At dawn, after a second night of sleeping out in frozen, rainswept open country, numb from the cold and with their outfits still stinking from their encounter with the entrail ditch, they had been ordered to wade across a swollen, dangerously fast river, holding their rifles above their heads as the water reached their chests. One man refused to cross and was instantly failed; another was swept away, rescued and then likewise failed. While both men were escorted to the waiting Bedfords, the others, though still wet and exhausted from contending with the river, were forced to carry one of their DS supervisors, complete with his bergen and weapons, between them on a stretcher for what should have been the last mile of the hike. However, when told at the end of that most killing of final legs that the Bedfords had gone and they would have to hike the last ten miles – in short, that they had been conned – some of them lost their temper with their supervisors, while others simply sat down wearily and called it a day.

The latter were failed and placed on RTU. A few more were lost on that draining ten miles, leaving a greatly reduced, less optimistic group to go on to the torments of Sickener Two.

'I mean, you can't believe what those fuckers will dream up for you, can you?' Jock asked rhetorically, really speaking to himself in a daze of disbelief as he thought back on all he had been through. 'You get through Sickener One, thinking you're Superman, then they promptly make you feel like a dog turd with Sickener Two. Those bastards sure have their talents!'

In fact, between the two exercises there had been more days of relentless grind in the shape of long runs, map-reading, survival and weapons training, and psychological testing. Then the dreaded first day of Sickener Two finally arrived, beginning with the horror of the Skirrid mountain, which rises 1640 feet above the gently rolling fields of Llanfihangel and is surmounted by a trig point ideal for map-reading. Naturally, for the SAS, the only way to the top was by foot, with the usual full complement of packed bergen, heavy webbing and weapons.

In addition, the route specially chosen by the DS for the exercise carefully avoided the gentler slopes and forced the candidates up the nearly vertical side. As part of the tests, each man had to take his turn at leading the others up the sheer face to the summit, using his Silvas compass, then guiding them back down without mistakes. This procedure was repeated many times throughout the long day, until each man had taken his turn as leader and all of them were suffering agonies of body and mind.

Some collapsed, some got lost through being dazed, and others simply dropped out in despair, while those remaining went on to week three. For this the teams were split up and each man was tested alone, with the runs becoming longer, the mountain routes steeper and the bergens packed more heavily every day until they became back-breaking loads. Added to this was an ever more relentless psychological onslaught, designed to test mental stamina, and including cruel psychological ploys such as last-minute changes of plan and awakenings at unexpected times of the day or night. On top of all this, even more brutal, unexpected physical endurance tests were introduced just as the men reached maximum exhaustion or disorientation.

The climax of this week of hell on earth was a repeated cross-graining of the peaks of the Pen-y-fan, at 2906 feet the highest mountain in the Brecon Beacons, one day after the other, each hike longer than the previous one, with extra weight being added to the bergens each time. On even the highest peak, the DS was liable to leap out of nowhere, and hurl a volley of questions at the exhausted, often dazed applicant, who, if he failed to supply an answer, would be sent back down in disgrace, bound for Platform Four.

By the fifth day of the third week, after a final, relentlessly punishing, 40 miles solo cross-graining of the bukits, known as the 'Fan Dance' – across icy rivers, peat bogs, pools of stagnant water and fields of fern; up sandstone paths and sheer ridges, in driving rain and blinding fog, carrying a 45lb bergen, as well as water bottles and heavy webbing – most of the candidates had been weeded out. In the end, under two dozen of the original hundred-odd men were deemed to have passed Initial Selection and allowed to go on to Continuation Training.

Phil Ricketts was one of them. He had had his moment of doubt on the summit of Pen-y-fan, when in a state of complete exhaustion, cold and hungry, whipped by the wind, feeling more alone than he had ever done before, he wanted to scream his protest and give up and go back down. But instead he endured and went on to do the rest of the nightmarish exercise and return to the RV by the selected route. He felt good when he finished and was applauded by his stern instructors.

Given a weekend break, Ricketts spent it with his wife in Wood Green, North London, where Maggie lived with her parents during his many absences from home. Even in the regular Army, he had never felt as fit as he was after Initial Selection, and he made love to Maggie, to whom he had only been married a year, with a passion that took her breath away. As they were to find out later, their first child, Anna, was conceived during that happy two days.

'You remember that first weekend break we got?' Ricketts asked his mates. 'Immediately after passing Initial Selection? What did you guys do that weekend?'

'I went back to Brixton,' Andrew said, 'to see my white Daddy and black Mammy, then screw my Scandinavian girlfriend. It was well worth the journey, believe me.'

'I banged a whore in King's Cross,' Jock said without emotion.

'Bill and I shared a hired car and drove back to the Midlands,' said Tom. 'Though my folks come from Wolverhampton they're now living in Smethwick, which isn't too far from where Bill lives, in Pensett. So since neither of us were keen to spend too much time with our families, we drove between the two towns, having a pint here, another pint there, and gradually getting pissed as newts.'

'I can hardly remember the drive back,' Bill said with a broad grin, 'so I like to think we only made it because of our SAS training. Who dares wins, and so on.'

16

'And you, Gumboot?' Ricketts asked. 'Did you go and see your wife?'

'No,' Gumboot answered, puffing smoke and sipping his beer at the same time.

'But you'd only been married six months,' Ricketts said.

'Six months too fucking long,' Gumboot said. 'Got her pregnant, didn't I? Besides, we only had one weekend, which leaves no time to go all the way to Devon and back.'

'You could have travelled on Friday night and come back on Sunday,' Andrew pointed out.

'OK, I'll admit it,' Gumboot said pugnaciously. 'I didn't want to spend my free weekend with a bloody bean bag, so I slipped into London. I'm amazed I didn't run into Jock, since I had a few pints in King's Cross on Saturday evening.'

'I probably saw you and avoided you,' Jock replied. 'I can be fussy at times.'

'Up yours, mate.' Gumboot swallowed some more beer, wiped his lips, and grinned mischievously. 'Ah, well, it was only a weekend – and over all too soon.'

On that, at least, they all agreed.

When they had returned to Hereford that Monday morning, some with blinding hangovers, others simply sleepless, they had been flung with merciless efficiency into their fourteen weeks of

Continuation Training, learning all the skills required to be a member of the basic SAS operational unit: the four-man patrol. These skills included weapons handling, combat and survival, reconnaissance, signals, demolitions, camouflage and concealment, resistance to interrogation, and first aid. Continuation Training was followed by jungle training and a static-line parachute course, bringing the complete programme up to six months.

Though Ricketts and the others had all come from regular Army, Royal Navy, RAF or Territorial Army regiments, and were therefore already fully trained soldiers, none of them was prepared for the amount of extra training they had to undergo with the SAS, even after the rigours of Initial Selection.

Weapons training covered everything in the SAS arsenal, including use of the standard-issue British semi-automatic Browning FN 9mm high-power handgun, the 9mm Walther PPK handgun, the M16 assault rifle, the self-loading semi-automatic rifle, or SLR, the Heckler & Koch MP5 sub-machine-gun, the MILAN anti-tank weapon, various mortars and a wide range of 'enemy' weapons, such as the Kalashnikov AK-47 assault rifle.

In combat and survival training they were taught the standard operating procedures, or

SOPs, for how to move tactically across country by day or night, how to set up and maintain observation posts, or OPs, and how to operate deep behind enemy lines. This led naturally to signals training, covering Morse code, special codes and call-sign systems, the operation of thirty kinds of SAS radio, recognition of radio 'black spots', the setting-up of standard and makeshift antennas, and the procedure for calling in artillery fire and air strikes.

As one of the main reasons for being behind enemy lines is the disruption of enemy communications and transportation, as well as general sabotage, particularly against Military Supply Routes, or MSRs, this phase of their training also included lessons in demolition skills and techniques, particularly the use of explosives such as TNT, dynamite, Semtex, Composition C3 and C4 plastic explosive, or PE, Amatol, Pentolite and Ednatol. Special emphasis was laid on the proper placement of charges to destroy various kinds of bridge: cantilever, spandrel arch, continuous-span truss and suspension.

Many jokes were made about the fact that those lessons led directly to instruction in first aid, including relatively advanced medical skills such as setting up an intravenous drip, how to administer drugs, both orally and with injections, and the basics of casualty handling and care.

This phase of Continuation Training culminated in escape and evasion (E&E) and Resistance to Interrogation (RTI) exercises. E&E began with a week of theory on how to live off the land by constructing makeshift shelters from branches, leaves and other local vegetation, and sangars, or semicircular shelters built from stones, and by catching and cooking wild animals. (Repeated jokes about rat stew, Ricketts recalled, had raised a few queasy laughs.) Those theories were then put into practice when the men were dropped off, alone, in some remote region, usually with no more than their clothing and a wristwatch, knife and box of matches, with orders to make their way back to a specified RV without either becoming lost or getting caught by the enthusiastic Parachute Regiment troopers sent out to find them.

Those caught were hooded, bound, thrown into the Paras' trucks and delivered to the interrogation centre run by the Joint Services Interrogation Unit and members of 22 SAS Training Wing, where various physical and mental torments were used to make them break down and reveal more than their rank, name, serial number and date of birth. Those who did so were failed even at that late stage in the course. Those who managed to remain sane and silent went on to undertake jungle-warfare training and the parachute course.

'For me,' Bill said, 'that was the best bit of all. I loved it in the jungle. I mean, even though it was tough all I could think of was how I'd come all the way from the Stevens and Williams Glassworks to the jungles of fucking Malaysia. I was in heaven, I tell you.'

'It wasn't Malaysia,' Andrew corrected him. 'It was just *close* to there. It's the only British dependency inhabited by Malays that didn't join the Federation of Malaysia.'

'He's so fucking educated,' Gumboot said, 'you'd never think he'd been up a tree. What the fuck's the difference? It was *jungle*, wasn't it? That's why you couldn't possibly fail there, mate. You must have felt right at home.'

'My family, comes from Barbados,' Andrew said, flashing Gumboot a big smile, 'where they have rum and molasses and white beaches. No jungle there, Gumboot.'

'Anyway,' Tom said, looking as solemn as always, 'I agree with Bill. I was a lot more relaxed when we went there. It was too late to fail, I thought.'

'So did some others,' Jock reminded them, 'and the poor bastards failed. One even failed during the parachute course. Can you fucking believe it?'

'That would have killed me,' Ricketts said. 'I mean, to be RTU'd at that stage. I would have opened a vein.'

'Hear, hear,' Andrew said.

Jungle-warfare training was a six-week course in Brunei, the British-protected sultanate of North-West Borneo, forming an enclave with Sarawak, Malaysia, where the SAS was reborn after World War Two and where it learnt so many of its skills and tactics. There the candidates were sent on four-man patrols through the jungle, some lasting almost a fortnight. During that time they had to carry out a number of operational tasks, including constructing a jungle basha, killing and eating wildlife, including snakes, without being bitten or poisoned, and living on local flora and fauna. Most importantly, they had to show that they could navigate and move accurately in the restricted visibility of the jungle. Failure in any of these tasks resulted in an even more cruel, last-minute, RTU.

Those who returned successfully from Brunei did so knowing that they had only one hurdle left: a four-week course at the No 1 Parachute Training School at RAF Brize Norton, Oxfordshire, where Parachute Jump Instructors, or PJIs, taught them the characteristics of PX1 Mk 4, PX1 Mk 5 and PR7 (reserve) parachutes, then supervised them on eight parachute jumps. The first of these was from a static balloon, but the others were from RAF C-130 Hercules aircraft, some from a high altitude, some from a low altitude, most by day, a few by night, and at least one while the aircraft was being put through a series of manoeuvres designed to shake up and disorientate the parachutists just before they jumped out. Those who made this final leap successfully had passed the whole course.

The men drinking around this table in the Paludrine Club had all just done that.

'I still don't believe it,' Andrew mused, 'but here we all are: in a Sabre Squadron at last. I think that's reason enough for another drink.'

'I think you're right,' Jock said, going off to the bar for another round.

Once badged, the successful candidates were divided between the four Sabre Squadrons, with those around this table going to Squadron B, where they would spend their probationary first year. They were also allowed into the Paludrine Club to celebrate their success and get to know each other as they had not been able to, or feared to, during the past six months of relentless training and testing.

'So,' Gumboot said, raising his glass when Jock

had set down the fresh round of drinks. 'Here's to all of us, lads.'

They touched their glasses together and drank deeply, trying not to look too proud.

2

The day after their celebratory booze-up with the other successful troopers, which was followed by a farewell fling with wives and girlfriends in the camp's Sports and Social Club, the six men allocated to B Squadron were called to the interest room to be given a briefing on their first legitimate SAS mission. As the group was so small, the briefing was not taking place in that room, but in the adjoining office of the Squadron Commander, Major Greenaway. To get to his office, however, the men had to pass through the interest room, which was indeed of interest, being dominated by a horned buffalo head set high on one wall and by the many photographs and memorabilia of previous B Squadron campaigns that covered the other walls, making the room look rather like a military museum.

Andrew was studying photographs of the Malaysia campaign, as well as items of jungle equipment, when a fair-haired SAS sergeant-major, built like a barrel but with no excess fat, appeared in the doorway of Major Greenaway's office.

'I'm your RSM,' he said. 'The name is Worthington, as befits a worthy man and don't ever forget it. Now step inside, lads.'

Following the Regimental Sergeant-Major into the office, they were surprised to find one wall completely covered by a blue curtain. Major Greenaway had silvery-grey hair and gazed up from behind his desk with keen, sky-blue eyes and a good-natured smile.

'You all know who I am,' he said, standing up by way of greeting, 'so I won't introduce myself. I would, however, like to offer you my congratulations on winning the badge and warmly welcome you to B Squadron.' When the men had murmured their appreciation, Greenaway nodded, turned to the wall behind him and pulled aside the blue curtain, revealing a large, four-colour map of the Strait of Hormuz, showing Muscat and Oman, with the latter boldly circled with red ink and the word 'SECRET' stencilled in bold black capital letters across the top.

Greenaway picked up a pointer and tapped the area marked 'Southern Dhofar'. 'Oman,' he said. 'An independent sultanate in eastern Arabia, located on the Gulf of Oman and the Arabian sea.

Approximately 82,000 square miles. Population 750,000 – mainly Arabs, but with substantial Negro blood. A medieval region, isolated from the more prosperous and advanced northern states by a 400-mile desert which rises up at its southern tip into an immense plateau, the Jebel Massif, a natural fortress some 3000 feet high, nine miles wide, and stretching 150 miles from the east down to, and across, the border with Aden, now the People's Democratic Republic of Yemen. The Gulf of Oman, about 300 miles long, lies between Oman and Iran, leading through the Strait of Hormuz to the Persian Gulf and the oil wealth of Saudia Arabia. So that's the place.'

The major lowered the pointer and turned back to face his new men. 'What's the situation?'

It was a rhetorical question requiring no answer other than that he was about to give. 'Oman has long-standing treaties of cooperation with Britain and is strategically important because Middle East oil flows to the West through the Strait of Hormuz. If the communists capture that oil, by capturing Oman, they'll end up controlling the economy of the Free World. The stakes, therefore, are high.'

Resting the pointer across his knees, Greenaway sat on the edge of his desk. Ricketts, who had worked on the North Sea oil rigs as a toolpusher before joining the regular Army, had been impressed by many of the men he met there: strong-willed, independent, decisive – basically decent. The 'boss', who struck him as being just such a man, went on: 'The situation in Oman has been degenerating since the 1950s with Sultan Said bin Taimur's repressive regime forcing more and more of the Dhofaris in the south – culturally and ethnically different from the people in the north – into rebellion. After turning against the Sultan, the rebels formed a political party, the Dhofar Liberation Front, or DLF, which the Sultan tried to quell with his Sultan's Armed Forces, or SAF. The rebels were then wooed and exploited by the pro-Soviet Yemenis, who formed them into the People's Front for the Liberation of the Occupied Arabian Gulf – the PFLOAG. This greatly improved the situation of the rebels, or *adoo*, and the Sultan's regime, falling apart, failed to mount an effective counter-insurgency war. Which is where we come in.'

He studied each of the men in turn, checking that he had their full attention and that they all understood him.

'What's "*adoo*" mean, boss?' Tom asked.

'It's the Arabic word for "enemy",' Greenaway informed him. 'Can I continue?'

'Yes, boss!'

'The SAF has long had a number of British ex-officers and NCOs as contract advisers, but

28

they were facing a losing battle in the countryside. Exceptionally cruel, punitive actions, such as the public hanging of suspected rebels and the sealing of their life-giving wells, were only turning more of the people against him. As it wasn't in British interests to let the communists take over Oman, in July last year the Sultan was overthrown by his son, Qaboos, in an almost bloodless coup secretly implemented and backed by us – by which I mean the British government, not the SAS.'

A few of the men laughed drily, causing the major to smile before continuing. 'However, while Qaboos, with our aid, gradually started winning the hearts of those ostracized by his father's reactionary regime, the PFLOAG – backed by the Russians, whose eyes are focused firmly on the oil-rich countries of Arabia – continued to make inroads into Oman. Now the *adoo* virtually control the Jebel Dhofar, which makes them a permanent threat to the whole country.'

Ricketts glanced at the other troopers and saw that they were as keen as he felt. What luck! Instead of Belfast, which was like Britain, only grimmer, they were going to fight their first war in an exotic, foreign country. Childish though it was, Ricketts could not help being excited about that. He had always needed changes of scenery, fresh challenges, new faces – which is why he had first gone to the North Sea, then joined the regular Army. While Belfast might have similar excitements, it was not the same thing. Ricketts was thrilled by the very idea of Oman, which remained a mysterious, perplexing country to all but a few insiders. Also, he was drawn to hot countries and desert terrain. Of course, Maggie would not be pleased and that made him feel slightly guilty. But he could not deny his true nature, which was to get up and go, no matter how much he loved his wife. He felt like a lucky man.

'What we're engaged in in Oman,' the boss continued, 'is the building of a bulwark against communist expansionism.' Standing again, he picked up the pointer and turned to the map. 'That bulwark will be Dhofar,' he continued, tapping the name with the pointer, 'in the south of Oman, immediately adjacent to communist-held Aden, now the People's Democratic Republic of Yemen. Our job is to back Sultan Qaboos with military aid and advice and to win the hearts of his people by setting up hospitals and schools, by teaching them the skills they need, and by crushing the *adoo* at the same time. The so-called hearts-and-minds campaign is already in progress, with British Army Training Teams, or BATT, based at Taqa and Mirbat. Our job is to tackle the *adoo*. Any questions so far?'

'Yes, boss,' Ricketts said, already familiar with SAS informality and determined to put it to good use. 'It's clearly a laudable aim, but how do we win the military side of it?'

Greenaway smiled. 'Not everyone considers our aims to be laudable, Trooper. Indeed, Britain has been accused of supporting a cruel, reactionary regime merely to protect its oil interests. While I happen to think that's the truth, I also believe it's justified. We must be pragmatic about certain matters, even when our motives aren't quite laudable.'

'Yes, boss,' Ricketts said, returning the major's wicked grin. 'So how do we fight the war, apart from winning hearts and minds?'

Greenaway put down the pointer, sat on the edge of the desk, and folded his arms. 'Since early last year, with the aid of the *firqats* – bands of Dhofari tribesmen loyal to the Sultan – we've managed to gain a few precarious toe-holds on the coastal plain immediately facing the Jebel Dhofar. Now, however, we're about to launch an operation designed to establish a firm base on the Jebel, from where we can stem the *adoo* advance. That operation is codenamed Jaguar.'

'Is this purely an SAS operation?' Andrew asked, realizing that this was a typical SAS 'Chinese parliament', or open discussion.

'No. In all matters relating to Oman, the SAF

and *firqats* must be seen to be their own men. For this reason, B Squadron and G Squadron will be supporting two companies of the SAF, Dhofari *firqats* and a platoon of Baluch Askars – tough little buggers from Baluchistan. Nearly 800 fighting men in all.'

'Are the SAF and the *firqats* dependable?' Gumboot asked, gaining the confidence to speak out like the others.

'Not always. The main problem lies with the *firqats*, who are volatile by nature and also bound by Islamic restrictions, such as the holy week of Ramadan, when they require a special dispensation to fight. But they have, on occasion, been known to ignore even that. When they fight, they can be ferocious, but they'll stop at any time for the most trivial reasons – usually arguments over who does what or gets what, or perhaps some imagined insult. So, no, they're not always dependable.'

'What about the *adoo*?' Ricketts asked.

'Fierce, committed fighters and legendary marksmen. They can pick a target off at 400 yards and virtually melt back into the mountainside or desert. A formidable enemy.'

'When does the assault on this Jebel what's-its-name begin?' Bill asked, nervously clearing his throat, but determined to be part of this Chinese parliament.

'About a month from now,' Greenaway

informed him. 'After you've all had a few weeks of training in local customs, language and general diplomacy, including seeing what previous SAS teams have been up to with schools, hospitals and so forth. It's anticipated that the assault on the . . .' – the major looked directly at Trooper Raglan with a tight little smile before pronouncing the name with theatrical precision – 'Jebel Dhofar will begin on 1 October. The Khareef monsoon, which covers the plateau with cloud and mist from June to September, will be finished by then, which will make the climb easier. Also, according to our intelligence, there'll be no moon that night, which should help to keep your presence unknown to the *adoo*.'

'Who, of course, have the eyes of night owls,' said Worthington, who had been standing silently behind them throughout the whole briefing. Only when Major Greenaway burst out laughing did the men realize that the RSM was joking. Still not quite used to SAS informality, some of them grinned sheepishly. Worthington managed to wipe the smiles from their faces by adding sadistically: 'Rumour has it that there are over 2000 *adoo* on the Jebel. That means the combined SAF and SAS forces will be outnumbered approximately three to one. Should any of you lads think those odds too high, I suggest you hand in your badges right now. Any takers?'

No one said a word, though some shook their heads. 'Good,' said the RSM, before turning his attention to Major Greenaway. 'Anything else, boss?'

'I think not, Sergeant-Major. This seems to be a healthy bunch of lads and I'm sure they'll stand firm.'

'I'm sure they will, boss.' The RSM looked grimly at the probationers. 'Go back to the spider and prepare your kit. We fly out tomorrow.'

'Yes, boss!' they all sang, practically in unison, then filed out of the office like excited schoolboys.

3

The four-engined Hercules C-130 took off the following afternoon from RAF Lyneham, refuelled at RAF Akroterion in Cyprus, then flew on to RAF Salalah in Dhofar, where the men disembarked by marching down the tailgate, from the gloom of the aircraft into the blinding, burning furnace of the Arabian sun.

On the runway of RAF Salalah stood Skymaster jets, each in its own sandbagged emplacement and covered by camouflage nets. Three large defensive trenches – encircled by 40-gallon drums and bristling with 25lb guns and 5.5 Howitzers, and therefore known as 'hedgehogs' – were laid out to the front and side of the airstrip. Overlooking all was an immense, sun-bleached mountain, its sheer sides rising dramatically to a plateau from the flat desert plain.

'That must be the Jebel Dhofar,' Ricketts said to Andrew.

'It is,' a blond-haired young man confirmed as

35

he clambered down from the Land Rover that had just driven up to the tailgate. 'And it's crawling with heavily-armed *adoo*. I'm Sergeant Frank Lampton, from one of the BATT teams. I'm here to guide you probationers through your first few days.' He grinned and glanced back over his shoulder at the towering slopes of the Jebel Dhofar, the summit of which was hazy with the heat. 'How'd you like to cross-grain the bukits of that?' he asked, turning back and grinning. 'Some challenge, eh?'

'It'd dwarf even the Pen-y-fan,' Andrew admitted. 'That's some mother, man.'

'Right,' Lampton said. Slim and of medium height, the sergeant was dressed in shorts, boots with rolled-down socks and a loose, flapping shirt, all of which were covered in the dust that was already starting to cover the new arrivals. A Browning 9mm high-power handgun was holstered on his hip. Squinting against the brilliant sunlight, he pointed to the convoy of armour-plated Bedfords lined up on the edge of the runway. 'Stretch your legs,' he told the men, 'and get used to the heat. When the QM has completed the unloading, pile into those trucks and you'll be driven to the base at Um al Gwarif. It's not very far.'

While the men gratefully did stretching exercises, walked about a bit or just sat on their bergens smoking, the Quartermaster Sergeant, a flamboyant Irishman with the lungs of a drill instructor, organized the unloading and sorting of all the squadron's kit by bawling good-natured abuse at his Omani helpers, all of whom wore *shemaghs* and the loose robes known as jellabas. The new arrivals watched them with interest.

'Fucked if I'd like to hump that stuff in *this* heat,' Gumboot finally said, breaking the silence.

'You soon will be,' Lampton replied with a grin, puffing smoke as he lit a cigarette. 'You'll be humping it up that bloody mountain, all the way to the top. That's why you'd better get used to the heat.' He inhaled and blew another cloud of smoke, then smiled wryly at Ricketts. 'Now these Omanis,' he said, indicating the men unloading the kit and humping it across to the Bedfords, 'they'd probably down tools if you asked them to do that. That's why they call the SAS "donkey soldiers" or *majnoons* – Arabic for "mad ones". Are they right or wrong, lads?'

'Anything you say, boss,' Bill said, 'is OK by me.'

'An obedient trooper,' Lampton replied, flicking ash to the ground. 'That's what I like to hear. Which one of you is Trooper Ricketts?' Ricketts put his hand in the air. 'I was informed by the

RSM that you're the oldest of the probationers,' Lampton said.

'I didn't know that, boss.'

'You're the oldest by one day, I was told, with Trooper McGregor coming right up your backside. That being the case, you'll be my second-in-command for the next few days. I trust you'll be able to shoulder this great responsibility.'

Lampton, though a sergeant, was hardly much older than Ricketts, who, feeling confident with him, returned his cocky grin. 'I'll do my best, boss.'

'I'm sure you will, Trooper. The RSM also said you put up a good show at the briefing. Fearless in the presence of your Squadron Commander. Right out front with the questions and so forth. That, also, is why you'll be in nominal charge of your fellow probationers while you're under my wing.'

'This sounds suspiciously like punishment, boss.'

'It isn't punishment and it isn't promotion – it's a mere convenience. Do you want to beg off?'

'No, boss.'

'You gave the correct answer, Trooper Ricketts. You're a man who'll go far.' Glancing towards the Bedfords, Lampton saw that Major Greenaway and RSM Worthington were already allocating the other members of B Squadron to their respective Bedfords. 'The unloading must be nearly completed,' Lampton said, dropping his cigarette butt to the tarmac and grinding it out with his heel. 'OK, Ricketts, collect the other probationers together and follow me to that truck.'

Ricketts did as he had been told, calling in his small group and then following Lampton across to one of the Bedfords parked on the edge of the airstrip. When they were in the rear, cramped together on the hard benches, already covered in a film of dust and being tormented by mosquitoes and fat flies, Lampton joined them, telling another soldier to drive his Land Rover back to base. The Bedford coughed into life, lurched forward, then headed away from the airstrip to a wired-off area containing a single-storey building guarded by local soldiers wearing red berets. The Bedford stopped there.

'SOAF HQ,' Lampton explained, meaning the Sultan of Oman's Air Force. Removing a fistful of documents from the belt of his shorts, he climbed down from the Bedford and went inside.

Forced to wait in the open rear of the crowded Bedford, Ricketts passed the time by examining the area beyond the SOAF HQ. He saw a lot of Strikemaster jet fighters and Skyvan cargo planes in dispersal bays made from empty oil drums.

The Strikemasters, he knew from his reading, were armed with Sura rockets, 500lb bombs and machine-guns. The Skyvan cargo planes would be used to resupply, or resup, the SAF and SAS forces when they were up on the plateau, which Ricketts could see in all its forbidding majesty, rising high above the plain of Salalah, spreading out from the camp's barbed-wire perimeter. The flat, sandy plain was constantly covered in gently drifting clouds of wind-blown dust.

Returning five minutes later with clearance to leave the air base, Lampton climbed back into the Bedford and told the driver to take off. After passing through gates guarded by RAF policemen armed with sub-machine-guns, the truck turned into the road, crossed and bounced off it, then headed along the adjoining rough terrain.

'What the matter with this clown of a driver?' Jock McGregor asked. 'The blind bastard's right off the road.'

'It's deliberate,' Lampton explained. 'Most of the roads in Dhofar have been mined by the *adoo*, so this is the safest way to drive, preferably following previous tyre tracks in case mines have been planted off the road as well. Of course, even that's no guarantee of safety. Knowing we do this, the *adoo* often disguise a mine by rolling an old tyre over it to make it look like the tracks of a previous truck. Smart cookies, the *adoo*.'

All eyes turned automatically towards the road, where the Bedford's wheels were churning up clouds of dust and leaving clear tracks.

'Great,' Gumboot said. 'You take one step outside your tent and get your fucking legs blown off.'

'As long as it leaves your balls,' Andrew said, 'you shouldn't complain, man.'

'Leave my balls out of this,' Gumboot said. 'You'll just put a curse on them.'

'Any other advice for us?' Ricketts asked.

'Yes,' Lampton replied. 'Never forget for a minute that the *adoo* are crack shots. They're also adept at keeping out of sight. The fact that you can't see them doesn't mean they're not there, and you won't find better snipers anywhere. You look across a flat piece of desert and think it's completely empty, then – pop! – suddenly a shot will ring out, compliments of an *adoo* sniper who's blended in with the scenery. They can make themselves invisible in this terrain – and they're bold as brass when it comes to infiltrating us. So never think you're safe because you're in your own territory. The truth is that you're never safe here. You've got to assume that *adoo* snipers are in the vicinity and keep your eyes peeled all the time.'

Again, they glanced automatically at the land they were passing through, seeing only the clouds of dust billowing up behind them, obscuring the sun-scorched flat plain and the immense, soaring sides of the Jebel Dhofar. The sky was a white sheet.

'Welcome to Oman,' Tom said sardonically. 'Land of sunshine and happy, smiling people. Paradise on earth.'

After turning off the road to Salalah, the truck bounced and rattled along the ground beside a dirt track skirting the airfield. About three miles farther on, it came to a large camp surrounded by a barbed-wire fence, with watch-towers placed at regular intervals around its perimeter. Each tower held a couple of armed SAF soldiers, a machine-gun and a searchlight. There were stone-built protective walls, or sangars, manned by RAF guards, on both sides of the main gate.

'This is Um al Gwarif, the HQ of the SAF,' Sergeant Lampton explained as the truck halted at the main gate. A local soldier wearing a green *shemagh* and armed with a 7.62mm FN rifle checked the driver's papers and then waved the Bedford through. The truck passed another watch-tower as it entered the camp. 'Home, sweet home, lads.'

Had it not been for the exotic old whitewashed fort, complete with ramparts and slitted windows, located near the centre of the enclosure and flying the triangular red-and-green Omani flag from its highest turret, the place might have been a concentration camp.

'That's the Wali's fort,' Lampton explained like a tour guide. 'That's W-A-L-I. Not wally as you know it. Here, a Wali isn't an idiot. He's the Governor of the province. So that's the Governor's fort, the camp's command post. And that,' he continued, pointing to an old pump house and well just inside the main gate, beyond one of the sangars, 'is where our running water comes from. Don't drink it unless you've taken your Paludrine. There, behind the well, to the right of those palm trees, is the officers' mess and accommodations.' He pointed to the lines of prefabricated huts located near the Wali's fort. 'Those are the barracks for the SAF forces. However, you lads, being of greater substance, are relegated to tents.'

He grinned broadly when the men let out loud moans.

As the Bedford headed for the eastern corner of the camp, Ricketts saw that many of the SAF men were gathering outside their barracks, most wearing the same uniform, but with a mixture of red, green, sand and grey berets.

'The SAF consists of four regiments,' Lampton explained. 'The Muscat Regiment, the Northern Frontier Regiment, the Desert Regiment and the Jebel Regiment. That, incidentally, is their order of superiority. While in the barracks, they can be distinguished from each other by their regimental beret. However, in the field they all wear a green, black and maroon patterned head-dress, known as a *shemagh*. As it's made of loose cloth and wraps around the face to protect the nose and mouth from dust, you'll all be given one to wear when you tackle the plateau.'

'We'll look like bloody Arabs,' Bill complained.

'No bad thing,' Lampton said. 'Incidentally, though there *are* a few Arab SAF officers, most of them are British — either seconded officers on loan from the British Army or contract officers.'

'You mean mercenaries,' Andrew objected.

'They prefer the term "contract officers" and don't you forget it.'

The Bedford came to a halt in a dusty clearing the size of a football pitch, containing two buildings: an armoury and a radio operations room. Everything else was in tents, shaded by palm trees and separated by defensive slit trenches. One of them was a large British Army marquee, used as the SAS basha, and off to the side were a number of bivouac tents.

The rest of the Bedfords had already arrived and were being unloaded as Ricketts and the others climbed out into fierce heat, drifting dust and buzzing clouds of flies and mosquitoes.

Once the all-important radio equipment had been stored in the radio ops room, they picked up their bergens and kit belts and selected one of the large bivouac tents, which contained, as they saw when they entered, only rows of camp-beds covered in mosquito netting and resting on the hard desert floor. After picking a spot, each man unrolled his sleeping bag, using his kit belt as a makeshift pillow. Already bitten repeatedly by mosquitoes, all the men were now also covered in what seemed to be a permanent film of dust.

Even as Ricketts was settling down between Andrew and Gumboot, Lampton came in to tell them that they only had thirty minutes for a rest. 'Then,' he said as they groaned melodramatically, 'you're to report to the British Army marquee, known here as the "hotel", for a briefing from the "green slime".' This mention of the Intelligence Corps provoked another bout of groans. When it had died down, Lampton added, grinning: 'And don't forget to take your Paludrine.'

'I hear those anti-malaria tablets actually *give* you malaria,' Bill said.

'Take them anyway,' Lampton said, then left them to their brief rest.

'What a fucking dump,' Gumboot said, lying back on his camp bed and waving the flies away from his face. 'Dust, flies and mosquitoes.'

'It's all experience,' Andrew said, tugging his

boots off and massaging his toes. 'Think of it as an exotic adventure. When you're old and grey, you'll be telling your kids about it, saying how great it was.'

'Exaggerating wildly,' Jock said from the other side of the tent. 'A big fish getting bigger.'

Ricketts popped a Paludrine tablet into his mouth and washed it down with a drink from his water bottle. Then, feeling restless, he stood up. 'No point in lying down for a miserable thirty minutes,' he said. 'It'll just make us more tired than we are now. Half an hour is long enough to get a beer. Who's coming with me?'

'Good idea,' Andrew said, heaving his massive bulk off his camp-bed.

'Me, too,' Gumboot said.

The rest followed suit and they all left the tent, walking the short distance to the large NAAFI tent and surprised to see a lot of frogs jumping about the dry, dusty ground. The NAAFI tent had a front wall of polyurethane cartons, originally the packing for weapons. Inside, there were a lot of six-foot tables and benches, at which some men were drinking beer, either from pint mugs or straight from the bottle. A shirtless young man smoking a pipe and sitting near the refrigerator introduced himself as Pete and said he was in charge of the canteen. He told them to help themselves, write their names and what they had had on the piece of paper on top of the fridge, and expect to be billed at the end of each month. All of them had a Tiger beer and sat at one of the tables.

'So what do you think of the place?' Pete asked them.

'Real exotic,' Gumboot said.

'It's not all that bad when you get used to it. I've been in worse holes.'

'Who else is here?' Ricketts asked.

'Spooks, Signals, BATT, Ordnance, REME, Catering Corps, Royal Corps of Transport, Engineers.'

'Spooks, meaning green slime,' Ricketts said.

'Yes. You're SAS, right?'

'Right.'

'They'll keep you busy here.'

'I hope so,' Andrew said. 'I wouldn't want to be bored in this hole. Time would stretch on for ever.'

'At least we've got outdoor movies,' Pete said, puffing clouds of smoke from his pipe. 'They're shown in the SAF camp. English movies one night, Indian ones the next. Just take a chair along with a bottle of beer and have yourself a good time. Me, I'm a movie buff.'

'I like books,' Andrew said. 'I write poetry, see? I always carry a little notebook with me and jot down my thoughts as they come to mind.'

'What thoughts?' Gumboot asked.

Andrew shrugged. 'Thoughts inspired by what I see and hear around me. I rewrite them in my head and jot them down.'

'You've got me in your notebook, have you?' Jock asked. 'All my brilliant remarks.'

'Ask no questions and I'll tell you no lies,' Andrew replied with a big grin. 'It's just poetry, man.'

'I didn't think you could spell,' Gumboot said, 'but maybe that doesn't matter.'

'Say, man,' Andrew said, taking a swipe at a dive-bombing hornet trying to get at his beer, 'how come there's so many frogs in this desert?'

'Don't know,' Pete said. 'But there's certainly a lot of 'em. Frogs, giant crickets, flying beetles, hornets, red and black ants, centipedes, camel spiders and scorpions – you name it, we've got it.'

'Jesus,' Tom said. 'Are any of those bastards poisonous?'

'The centipedes and scorpions can give you a pretty serious sting, so I'd recommend you shake out anything loose before picking it up. Those things like sheltering beneath clothes. They like to hide in boots and shoes. So never pick *anything* up without shaking it out first.'

'What about the spiders?' Bill asked, looking uneasy.

'They look pretty horrible, but they don't bite.

One has a small body and long legs, the other short legs and a big, fat body. You'll find them all over the bloody place, including under your bedclothes – another reason for shaking everything out.'

Bill shivered at the very thought of the monsters. 'I *hate* spiders!' he said.

The thunder of 25-pounder guns suddenly shook the tent, taking everyone by surprise.

'Christ!' Jock exclaimed. 'Are we being attacked?'

'No,' Pete said. 'It's just the SAF firing on the Jebel from the gun emplacements just outside the wire. You'll get that at regular intervals during the day and even throughout the night, disturbing your sleep. It's our way of deterring the *adoo* hiding in the wadis from coming down off the Jebel. It takes some getting used to, but eventually you *will* get used to it – that and the croaking of the bloody frogs, which also goes on all night.'

'Time for our briefing,' Ricketts said. 'Drink up and let's go, lads.' They all downed their beer, thanked Pete, and left the tent. Once outside, Ricketts looked beyond the wire and saw one of the big guns firing from inside its protective ring of 40-gallon drums, located about a hundred yards outside the fence. The noise was tremendous, with smoke and flame belching out of the long barrel. The backblast made dust billow up around the Omani gunners, who had covered their ears with their hands to keep out the noise.

'That's one hell of a racket to get used to,' Jock said.

'Plug your ears,' Gumboot told him.

The briefing took place in the corner of the marquee known as the 'hotel', where Sergeant Lampton was waiting for them, standing beside another man who, like Lampton, was wearing only a plain shirt, shorts and slippers.

'Welcome to Um al Gwarif,' he said. 'I'm Captain Ralph Banks of SAS Intelligence and I don't like to hear the term "green slime".' When the laughter had died down, he continued: 'You may have noticed that I'm not wearing my green beret or insignia. You may also have noticed that everyone else around here is like me – no beret, no insignia. There's a good reason for it. While we're all here at the Sultan's invitation, there are those, both here and in Great Britain, who would disapprove of our presence here, so to avoid identification we don't wear cap badges, identification discs, badges of rank or formation signs. This also means that the *adoo* won't know who we are if they capture us, dead or alive. Of course, if they capture you alive, they may try some friendly persuasion, in which case we trust that your interrogation training will stand you in good stead.'

The men glanced at one another, some grinning sheepishly, then returned their attention to the 'Head Shed', as senior officers were known.

'I believe you were briefed in Hereford,' he said, 'about the general situation here in Oman.'

'Yes, boss,' some of the men replied.

'Good. What I would like to fill you in on is what you'll be doing for the next few days, before we make the assault on the Jebel Dhofar and start ousting the *adoo*.' Banks turned to the map behind him. 'As you've already been informed, everything that happens here must be seen to be the doing of the Omanis. With our help, the Sultan's Armed Forces have established bases all around this area. At Taqa,' he said, pointing the names out on the map, 'Mirbat and Sudh, all on the coast, and also here in the western area at Akoot, Rayzut, where a new harbour is being built, at Thamrait, or Midway, on the edge of the Empty Quarter, and even on the Jebel itself, at the Mahazair Pools, which will be your first RV when the assault begins.' He turned back to face them. 'While the next military objective is the assault on the Jebel, it's imperative that you men first learn about the workings of the BATT, who assist the SAF with training, advice and community welfare. Also, before you make the assault on the Jebel you'll have to learn how to deal with the *firqats*, who can be a prickly, unpredictable bunch.'

He nodded at Sergeant Lampton, who took over the briefing. 'The *firqats* are irregular troops formed into small bands led by us. Many of them are former *adoo* who sided with Sultan Qaboos when he deposed his father and started his reforms. As they know the *adoo* camps and bases, those particular *firqats* are very useful, but they aren't overly fond of the Sultan's regular army and, as Captain Banks said, they can be very difficult to deal with. For this reason, part of the work of the BATT teams is to be seen doing good deeds, as it were, in the countryside, thus impressing the *firqats* with our general worthiness and strengthening their support for the Sultan. So it's imperative that you learn exactly what the BATT teams are doing and how they go about doing it. Therefore, for your first week here, you'll be split up into small teams, each led by a BATT man, including myself, and given a guided tour of the area, plus special training relating to warfare in this particular environment. At the end of that week, the assault on the Jebel will commence. Any questions?'

There was a brief silence, broken only when Ricketts asked: 'When do we start?'

'Tomorrow morning. You have the rest of the day off. As the sun is due to sink shortly, it won't be a long day. Any more questions?'

As there were no further questions, the group was disbanded and went off to the open mess tent to have dinner at the trestle tables. Afterwards they returned to the NAAFI tent to put in a solid evening's drinking, returning at midnight, drunk and exhausted, to their bivouac tent. After nervously shaking out their kit to check for scorpions and centipedes, they wriggled into their sleeping bags for what was to prove a restless night punctuated by croaking frogs, irregular blasts from the 25-pounders and attacks by thirsty mosquitoes and dive-bombing hornets. Few of the men felt up to much the next day, but they still had their work to do.

4

For the next five days, Ricketts, Andrew and
Gumboot were driven around the area in
Lampton's Land Rover, with Ricketts driving,
the sergeant beside him and the other two in
the back with strict instructions to keep their
eyes peeled at all times. To ensure that they
did not dehydrate, they had brought along a
plentiful supply of water bottles and *chajugles*,
small canvas sacks, rather like goatskins, that
could be filled with water and hung outside the
vehicle to stay cool. Just as the Bedfords had done
the first day, Ricketts always drove alongside the
roads, rather than on them, to minimize the risk
from land-mines laid by the *adoo*.

The heat was usually fierce, from a sky that
often seemed white, but they gradually got used
to it, or at least learned to accept it, and they
frequently found relief when they drove along
the beaches, by the rushing surf and white
waves of the turquoise sea. The beaches, they

soon discovered, were covered with crabs and lined with wind-blown palm trees. Beyond the trees, soaring up to the white-blue sky, was the towering gravel plateau of the Jebel Dhofar, a constant reminder that soon they would have to climb it – a daunting thought for even the hardiest.

As they drove through the main gates that first morning, the big guns in the hedgehogs just outside the perimeter fired on the Jebel, creating an almighty row, streams of grey smoke and billowing clouds of dust. Just ahead of their Land Rover, a Saladin armoured car was setting out across the dusty plain, right into the clouds of dust.

'The *adoo* often mount small raids against us,' Lampton explained. 'They also come down from the Jebel during the night to plant mines around the base or dig themselves in for a bit of sniping. That *Saladin* goes out every morning at this time to sweep the surrounding tracks, clear any mines left and keep an eye out for newly arrived *adoo* snipers. The same procedure takes place at RAF Salalah, which is where we're going right now.'

Reversing the same three-mile journey they had made the day before, when they first arrived, with the Land Rover bouncing constantly over the rough gravel-and-sand terrain beside the dirt track, they soon passed the guarded perimeter of RAF Salalah, then came to the main gate by the single-storey SOAF HQ. Their papers were checked by an Omani soldier wearing the red beret of the Muscat Regiment and armed with a 7.62mm FN rifle. Satisfied, he let them drive through the gates and on to where the Strikemaster jets and Skyvan cargo planes were being serviced in the dispersal bays encircled by empty oil drums.

'Stop right by that open Skyvan,' Lampton said. When Ricketts had done so, they all climbed down. Lampton introduced them to a dark-haired man wearing only shorts and slippers, whose broad chest and muscular arms were covered in sweat. Though he was wearing no shirt, he carried a Browning 9mm high-power handgun in a holster at his hip. He was supervising the loading of heavy resup bundles into the cargo bay in the rear of the Skyvan. The heavy work was being done by other RAF loadmasters, all of whom were also stripped to the waist and gleaming with sweat.

'Hi, Whistler,' Lampton said. 'How are things?'

'No sweat,' Whistler replied.

'You're *covered* in bloody sweat!'

Whistler grinned. 'No sweat otherwise.' He glanced at the men standing around Lampton. 'These bullshit artists have just been badged,' Lampton said, by way of introduction, 'and are starting their year's probationary with us. Men, this is Corporal Harry Whistler of 55 Air Despatch Squadron, Royal Corps of Transport. Though he's normally based on Thorney Island and was recently on a three-month tour of detachment to the army camp in Muharraq, he's here to give us resup support. As his surname's "Whistler" and he actually whistles a lot, we just call him . . .'

'Whistler,' Andrew said.

'What a bright boy you are.'

Everyone said hello to Whistler. 'Welcome to the dustbowl,' he replied 'I'm sure you'll have a great time here.'

'A real holiday,' Gumboot said.

'You won't be seeing too much of Whistler,' Lampton told them, 'because he'll usually be in the sky directly above you, dropping supplies from his trusty Skyvan.'

Grinning, Whistler glanced up at the semi-naked loadmasters, who were now inside the cargo hold, lashing the bundles to the floor with webbing freight straps and 1200lb-breaking-strain cords.

'What's in the bundles?' Rickets asked.

'Eighty-one-millimetre mortar bombs, HE phosphorus and smoke grenades, 7.62mm ball and belt ammo, compo rations, water in jerrycans — four to a bundle. Those are for the drops to our troopers at places like Simba, Akoot and Jibjat, but we also have food resup for the *firqats* out in the field, since those bastards are quick to go on strike if they think we're ignoring them.' Whistler pointed to some bundles wrapped in plastic parachute bags for extra protection. 'Tins of curried mutton or fish, rice, flour, spices, dates, and the bloody oil used for the cooking, carried in tins that always burst – hence the parachute bags. As well as all that, we drop the propaganda leaflets that are part of the hearts-and-minds campaign. It's like being a flying library for the illiterate.'

'Whistler will also be helping out now and then with a few bombing raids,' Lampton informed them, 'though not with your regular weapons, since those are left to the Strikemaster jets.'

'Right,' Whistler said. 'We're already preparing for the assault on the Jebel.' He pointed to the six 40-gallon drums lined up on the perimeter track by the runway. 'We're going to drop those on the Jebel this afternoon, hopefully on some dumbstruck *adoo*, as a trial run.'

'What are they?' Ricketts asked.

'Our home-made incendiary bombs. We call them Burmail bombs.'

'They look like ordinary drums of aviation oil.'

'That's just what they are – drums of Avtur. But we dissolve polyurethane in the Avtur to thicken it up a bit; then we seal the drums, fix Schermuly flares to each side of them, fit them with cruciform harnesses and roll them out the back of the Skyvan. They cause a hell of an explosion, lads. Lots of fire and smoke. We use them mainly for burning fields that look like they've been cultivated by the *adoo*. However, if help is required by you lads on the ground, but not available from the Strikemasters, we use the Burmail bombs against the *adoo* themselves.'

'Why are they called Burmails?' asked Andrew, a man with a genuine fondness for words.

'"Burmail" is an Arabic word for oil drums,' Whistler told him. 'Thought by some to be a derivation from Burmah Oil, or the Burmah Oil Company.'

'What's it like flying in on an attack in one of those bathtubs?' Gumboot asked with his customary lack of subtlety.

'Piece of piss,' Whistler replied, unperturbed. 'We cruise in at the minimum safe altitude of 7000 feet, then lose altitude until we're as low as 500 feet, which we are when we fly right through the wadis on the run in to the DZ. When those fucking Burmail bombs go off, it's like the whole world exploding. So anytime you need help, just call. That's what we're here for, lads.'

*   *   *

On the second day Lampton made Ricketts drive them out to the Salalah plain, where they saw Jebalis taking care of small herds of cattle or carrying their wares, mostly firewood, on camels, en route to Salalah. This reminded the troopers that life here continued as normal; that not only the *adoo* populated the slopes of the Jebel Dhofar and the arid sand plain in front of it.

That afternoon the group arrived at the old walled town of Salalah. At the main gate they had to wait for ages while the Sultan's armed guards, the Askouris, searched through the bundles of firewood on the Jebalis' camels to make sure that their owners were not smuggling arms for the *adoo* supporters inside the town, of which there were known to be a few. Eventually, when the camels had passed through, the soldiers' papers were checked, and they were allowed to drive into the town, along a straight track that led through a cluster of mud huts to an oasis of palm trees, lush green grass and running water. They passed the large jail to arrive at the Sultan's white, fortified palace, where Lampton made Ricketts stop.

'When Sultan Sa'id Tamur lived there,' Lampton recounted, 'he was like a recluse, shunning all Western influence, living strictly by the Koran and ruling the country like a medieval despot. Though his son, Qaboos, was trained at Sandhurst, when he returned here he was virtually kept a prisoner – until he deposed his old man at gunpoint, then sent him into exile in London. He died in the Dorchester Hotel in 1972. A nice way to go.'

'And by reversing his father's despotism,' Andrew said from the back of the Land Rover, 'Qaboos has gradually been finding favour with the locals.'

'With our help, yes. He's been particularly good at increasing recruitment to the army and air force. He's also built schools and hospitals, plus a radio station whose specific purpose is to combat communist propaganda from Radio Aden. He's trying to bring Oman into the twentieth century, but I doubt that he'll get that far. However, if he wins the support of his people and keeps the communists out of Oman, we'll be content.'

'Our oil being protected,' put in Ricketts.

'That's right,' Lampton said. 'Wait here. I'm going in to give Qaboos a written report on recent events. He likes to be kept informed. When I come out, I'll give you a quick tour of the town.'

'It's more like a bleedin' village,' Gumboot complained.

'It might be a village in Devon,' Lampton said as he got out of the vehicle, 'but here it's a town. Relax, lads. Put your feet up. This could take some time.'

In fact, it took nearly two hours. While Lampton was away, Ricketts and the other two had a smoke, repeatedly quenched their thirst with water from the water bottles and *chajugles*, and gradually became covered in a slimy film composed of sweat and dust. Already warned to neither stare at, nor talk to, the veiled women who passed by with lowered heads, they amused themselves instead by making faces at some giggling local kids, giving others chewing gum, and practising their basic Arabic with the gendarmes who were indifferently guarding the Sultan's palace, armed with .303 Short-Magazine Lee Enfield, or SMLE, rifles. When Lampton emerged and again offered them a quick tour of the town, they politely refused.

'We've seen all there is to see,' Gumboot said, 'and we're frying out here, boss. Can we go somewhere cooler?'

Lampton grinned as he took his seat in the Land Rover. 'OK, lads. Let's go and see some of the BATT handiwork. That'll take us along the seashore and help cool you down.'

He guided Ricketts back out through the walled town's main gates and down to the shore, then made him head for Taqa, halfway between Salalah and Mirbat. The drive did indeed take them along the shore, with the ravishing turquoise sea on one side and rows of palm and date trees on the other. A cool breeze made the journey pleasant, though Ricketts had to be careful not to get stuck in the sand. Also, as he had noticed before, there were a great many crabs, in places in their hundreds, scuttling in both directions across the beach like monstrous ants and being crushed under the wheels of the Land Rover.

'I get the shivers just looking at 'em,' Gumboot told them while visibly shivering in the rear of the Land Rover. 'I'd rather fight the *adoo*.'

'There's a BATT station at Taqa,' Lampton said, oblivious to the masses of crabs, 'so you can see the kind of work we do there. You know, of course, that the SAS has been in Oman before.'

'I didn't know that,' Gumboot said to distract himself from the crabs. 'But then I'm pig-ignorant, boss.'

'I know they were here before,' Andrew said, 'but I don't know why.'

'He's pig-ignorant as well,' Gumboot said. 'Now I don't feel so lonely.'

'It was because of Britain's treaty obligations to Muscat and Oman,' Lampton informed them. 'In the late 1950s we were drawn into a counter-insurgency campaign when the Sultan's regime was threatened by a rebellious army of expatriate Omanis from Saudi Arabia. As their first major move against the Sultan, they took over the Jebel Akhdar, or Green Mountain, in the north of Oman, and declared the region independent from him.'

'Which did not amuse him greatly,' Andrew said.

'Definitely not,' Lampton replied. 'We Brits were called in to help. When British infantry, brought in from Kenya in 1957, failed to dislodge the rebels from the mountain, D Squadron and A Squadron of 22 SAS were flown in to solve the problem. In January 1959 they made their legendary assault on the Jebel Akhdar, winning it back from the rebels. Once they had done that, they implemented the first hearts-and-minds campaign to turn the rest of the locals into firm supporters of the Sultan. Unfortunately, with his medieval ways, Sultan Qaboos's old man undid all the good done by the SAS. Now Qaboos has another rebellion on his hands.'

'Which is why we're here,' Andrew said.

'Yes. What we did in 1959, we're going to have to do again twelve years later: engage in another hearts-and-minds campaign, while also defeating the *adoo* on the Jebel Dhofar.'

'What exactly does a hearts-and-minds campaign involve?' Ricketts asked him.

'The concept was first devised in Malaya in the early 1950s and used successfully in Borneo from 1963 to 1966. It's now an integral part of our counter-insurgency warfare methods. Its basic thrust is to gain the trust of the locals of any given area by sharing their lifestyle, language and customs. That's why, for instance, in Borneo, SAS troopers actually lived with the natives in the jungle, assisting them with their everyday needs and providing medical care. In fact, medical care is one of the prime tools in the hearts-and-minds campaign. We even train some of the BATT men in midwifery and dentistry. Those skills, along with basic education, building small schools and hospitals, and teaching crafts that create work, have won us lots of friends in many regions.'

'Fucked if I'd deliver a baby,' Gumboot said. 'There's a limit to duty.'

'You'd be surprised at the number of SAS men who've delivered babies and pulled teeth in emergencies.' Lampton turned to Ricketts. 'Watch out for the water here. This bay leads to Taqa.'

Even as Lampton was speaking, the Land Rover was driving into the shallow water of a bay surrounded by small cliffs. By using four-wheel drive, Ricketts got them across to dry land, where they passed more cliffs and sand dunes, before arriving at another beach. There, flocks of seagulls were winging repeatedly over piles of rotten, stinking fish that were scattered between the beached fishing boats. After passing the boats and the Arab fishermen sitting in them repairing the nets, they arrived at a small village of mud huts. At the end of its single, dusty street were two buildings taller than the others, being three storeys high, with the Omani flag flying from one of them.

'Taqa,' Lampton said. 'Stop here.' Ricketts pulled up, then followed the others out of the vehicle. 'The building with the flag,' Lampton told them, 'is the Wali's house. The other tall building is the BATT house. Now let's meet the BATT men.'

Three of the latter were on the first floor of the BATT house, brewing tea on a No 1 burner and placing tin mugs on the trestle table that took up most of the tiny room. The shelves were stacked with tins of compo rations and cooking utensils, indicating that the room was used as a combined kitchen and mess room. SLR and M16 rifles were piled up in a corner, along with boxes of grenades, webbing, phosphorus flares and other ammunition.

When introductions had been made, the tea was poured and the BATT men, constantly interrupting one another, explained that they were still working to win the hearts and minds of the villagers. They were having problems, however, because some of the men of the village were suspected of belonging to the *adoo* – for they often disappeared for weeks at a time – and the villagers, including the Wali, were worried about possible reprisals against them once the BATT teams moved out.

'So one of our jobs,' Corporal Roy Coleman said, 'is to persuade the villagers that we won't be leaving until the *adoo* have been defeated militarily and forced off the Jebel once and for all. Another problem is that these villagers are still pretty primitive, and although we give them medical treatment we're up against a lot of their old beliefs and superstitions.'

'Is this the whole BATT team?' Ricketts asked, indicating the three troopers with a nod of his head.

'No. There's eight of us. Some are sleeping, a couple are in the Wali's fort, keeping their ear to the radio, and the rest are performing their duties in the village. Let's go outside and see what's happening. If you hear gunshots, don't worry. We're giving firing lessons to some of the gendarmes on a makeshift firing range on the beach. It's not the *adoo*.'

Leaving the house, Coleman led them to the back of the building, where a tent had been set up as a basic, open-air surgery. Gunshots did indeed ring out from the direction of the beach as they approached the Omanis queuing for medical treatment at the tent. The SAS medic was standing behind a trestle table, sweating in the afternoon heat as he went about his work. Introduced to the probationers, he talked to them as he continued cleaning and bandaging cuts, lancing boils, treating bad burns and dispensing a wide variety of tablets.

'Some of the tablets are genuine and some are piss-takes,' he said. 'You get hypochondriacs even in this place, believe me. I was trained at the US Army's special forces medical school at Fort Sam, in Houston, and Fort Bragg, North Carolina – the best of its kind – which means that although I'm not a doctor I can deal with just about anything short of major surgery. Here, the most common problems are boils, burns, ruptures, messed-up circumcisions, conjunctivitis, dysentery, malaria, yellow fever, sand-fly fever and dengue from mosquitoes . . .'

'Don't tell me!' Gumboot interrupted sardonically.

'. . . trench fever from lice, spotted fever from ticks, every kind of typhus, even leprosy and the dire results of floggings ordered by the Wali. Like the other medics, if I come across something I can't handle I simply call the BATT doctor at Um al Gwarif. Nevertheless, I have two major problems. One is being up against the primitive practices of the local witch doctors, who tend to cure all ills by branding the pained area with a red-hot iron. The other is trying to work out which of the villagers are really sick and which are just becoming pill heads. Gradually, however, more and more of them are coming to depend increasingly on us while rejecting the advances of the *adoo*. That's the whole point.'

'It's also the point of the school we've recently built for them,' Coleman said as he led them away from the medical tent, 'and for the firing practice we give to the gendarmes. The more we give them, the less they appreciate the *adoo*. And that, in a nutshell, is what's known as the hearts-and-minds campaign.'

The following day they were at Mirbat, on the south coast of Dhofar. It was little more than a collection of dusty mud huts and clay buildings, with the sea on one side and a protective barbed-wire fence running north and east. The settlement included a cluster of houses to the south; a market by the sea; some thirty armed Omanis, housed in an ancient Wali's fort to the west; another small fort about 500 yards to the west, holding 25 men of the Dhofar Gendarmerie, or DG; and, near the market in the middle of the compound, a mud-built BATT house holding nine BATT men under the command of the 23-year-old Captain Mike Kealy. Eight hundred yards north of the northern perimeter, on the slopes of Jebel Ali, was another Dhofar Gendarmerie outpost.

'We've won the hearts and minds of this town,' Captain Kealy informed them, 'but the *adoo* harass us all the time and, so it's rumoured, are determined to capture the town and wipe out the defenders as an inspiration to their own wavering troops and a warning to all those who oppose them.'

'What kind of defences do you have?' Ricketts asked him.

'You mean, apart from the men?'

'Yes.'

Kealy shrugged. 'Not much. The only heavy weapons are an old 25-pounder in a gun-pit next to the DG fort, a single 7.62mm GPMG on the BATT house roof, an 81mm mortar emplaced beside the building and a 0.5in-calibre heavy machine gun.' Kealy shrugged again. 'That's it.'

'That's not much.'

'If they come,' Kealy said, 'we'll be waiting for them. Don't doubt that, Trooper.'

'I won't,' Ricketts replied.

Leaving the BATT house, they were introduced to other members of B Squadron, including three Fijians – the enormous Corporal Labalaba, known as Laba, Valdez, and Sekonia, known as Sek. They were told that all three had joined up during the British Army's major recruitment drive in Fiji and were veterans of the Keeni Meeni operations in Aden, as well as later missions in Borneo.

'What's "Keeni Meeni" mean?' Gumboot asked, almost tripping over his own tongue.

The enormous Labalaba, who was even taller than Andrew, looked down at Gumboot and grinned. 'Keeni Meeni? It's a Swahili phrase used to describe the movement of a snake in the grass. In Aden we'd disguise ourselves as Arabs, infiltrate our chosen district and seek out the enemy, quickly pull our Browning handguns from our *futahs*, the traditional Arab robes, neutralize the enemy with a "double-tap", then melt back into the scenery – just like snakes in the grass!'

'You mean, you'd blow the poor fucker away.'

'You've got it, Trooper.'

Leaving the sandbagged gun-pit, where the three Fijians had been cleaning the big gun, they saw their first *firqats*, just down from the hills and returning their FN rifles and other weapons to the armoury in the Wali's fort. Though they all had similar *shemaghs*, the rest of their clothing was widely varied, ranging from the loose robes worn by most locals to Khaki Drill (KD), or Light Tropical, uniforms. Festooned with webbing, ponchos and bandoliers of ammunition, and with the large Omani knives called *kunjias* tied around their waists, they looked like a particularly fierce band of brigands.

'I wouldn't like to fucking tangle with them,' Gumboot said admiringly.

'Don't,' warned Lampton. 'They're extremely efficient with those knives and quick to use them. Only last year, they murdered a British officer in his tent when he refused to give them what they wanted. And those men, believe it or not, are the ones you depend on. Now let's get back to the basha and have a couple of cooling beers.'

'The word's *soothing*,' Andrew corrected him, glancing back over his shoulder at the fierce-looking *firqats*. 'Let's all go for a *soothing* beer.'

They drove gratefully back to base.

5

The indoctrination tour continued. Lampton had Ricketts drive them to Rayzut, where British Army engineers were constructing a new harbour from large blocks raised around the bay and an SAS BATT team was inoculating the local labour force. Many of the latter, Ricketts noticed, were so intrigued by modern medicine that they queued up eagerly to have their jabs.

At Arzat, which was little more than a random collection of mud huts with a small garrison of Dhofar Gendarmerie, they found an SAS BATT team showing the locals how to purify the water tanks with fluoride and transform their rubbish into fuel. SAS veterinary surgeons were also present, showing the locals how to improve the breeding of their cattle and training them in basic veterinary medicine.

At Janook, the probationers were given an enthusiastic lecture by a four-man BATT 'Psyops' team, formerly of the Northern Ireland regiments and now responsible for Psychological Operations in Oman. These activities included, apart from the writing of the propaganda leaflets dropped from the Skyvans, the showing of British and Hollywood movies to the locals.

'The theory,' they were informed by Corporal Hamlyn of the BATT team, 'is that with little or no command of English, the locals can receive the benefits of Western civilization more easily from moving images than they can from the printed page.'

'Never attack the written word,' Andrew said, jotting some in his notebook, presumably for future poems. 'There are aspects of humanity that the moving image can never describe.'

The corporal looked up in surprise at the immense black newcomer. 'What's that, Trooper? I'm not sure I heard that right.'

'The moving image is severely limited in its payload. It's the printed word that will always knock 'em out.'

'Not in this case, Trooper. These folk in their jellabas and *shemaghs* don't speak any English, so it's easier to show them some movies, preferably action-packed.'

'Charles Bronson,' Gumboot said.

'Clint Eastwood,' Ricketts added.

'I'm with you,' Andrew said. 'Movies that

demonstrate Democracy in action – lots of guns and dead bodies.'

'Are you taking the piss, Trooper?'

'Just bouncing a few ideas, Corporal.'

'He's just stopped living off bananas,' Gumboot explained, 'and has withdrawal symptoms.'

'Piss off, you lot,' Hamlyn said.

Andrew was more impressed when, at Suda, another windswept, dusty village scattered around a lovely bay on the Arabian Sea, they spent some time with a BATT team who were teaching the local children English with the aid of carefully selected illustrated books that showed them the wealth and wonders of the West – none of which, the BATT team repeatedly emphasized to their impressionable pupils, would be supplied by the communists.

'See what I mean?' Andrew said triumphantly. 'When it really gets down to the nitty-gritty, the printed word is what matters.'

'Not forgetting the pretty pictures,' Gumboot reminded him.

'They're only there to support the words.'

'Every kid I saw was looking at the pictures,' Ricketts chipped in. 'Not reading the words.'

'A mere diversion,' Andrew insisted. 'They were merely stopping to think a bit. The pictures visually confirmed what the words had conveyed to them, but it's the words, not the pictures, that they'll be able to use in the future. We're talking language here, man!'

'That's quite a mouthful, Andrew.'

'It's verbal diarrhoea,' Gumboot insisted, 'caused by all those bananas.'

'Better than mental constipation,' Andrew retorted, 'of the kind you know so well.'

'Cut out the bullshit,' Lampton said. 'These matters are serious. The point is that whether with pictures or prose, movies or chewing gum, we're showing these people what they can have if they side with us instead of the communists. Call it brainwashing if you like, but that's what we're about here.'

Finally, during the late afternoon of their fourth day, Lampton guided Ricketts – still driving while Andrew and Gumboot kept a constant watch for *adoo* snipers – to a desolate village located in rough, gravel flatland west of the Jebel Dhofar, in a region once patrolled by the rebels but now back in the hands of the SAF.

'Never forget,' Lampton told them as they approached the village in four-wheel drive, bouncing over the rough, rocky ground, 'that the *adoo* are fanatical communists, backed by the Soviet Union and the Chinese. Often removed from their parents to be schooled in the PDRY – the People's Democratic Republic of Yemen, formerly Aden – or sent to guerrilla-warfare schools in Russia and China, they're returned to their mountain villages as fanatics. There they establish communist cells, breaking down former loyalties, organizing their converts first into village militias, then into seasoned battle groups who show absolutely no mercy to the Muslims. They ban all religious practices, torture village elders into denying their faith and routinely rape their women. In other words, they're engaged in a campaign of terror designed to wipe out Islam altogether and establish communism in Oman – and they're ruthless in doing it.'

The Land Rover bounced down off the rough ground on the lower slopes of the Jebel, then travelled along the flat gravel plain until it arrived at a dusty village of clay huts, Arabs in traditional dress and a surprising variety of animals, including cattle, mountain goats, mangy dogs and chickens.

The sun was just beginning to sink, casting great shadows over the village, when Lampton told Ricketts to stop the Land Rover near the two wells, where a group of SAS men had gathered. Explosive charges, detonating cords, primers and other demolition equipment could be seen in opened boxes on the ground by their feet.

'Are those sappers?' Andrew asked.

'Yes,' Lampton replied. 'Under the command of one of our demolition specialists.'

As Lampton climbed out of the Land Rover and approached the men around one of the wells, followed by the others, the men, in two groups, both being watched attentively by many villagers, including children, were leaning over the walls of the two wells and shouting down into them. The voices of men down inside the wells came back up with a hollow, reverberating quality, though what they said could not be made out.

'You look like you're ready to take a dive,' Lampton said, stopping just behind one of the men leaning over the bricked parapet of the well. 'What's going on?'

The man straightened up and turned around to gaze at Lampton. He had unkempt red hair, a beakish, broken nose, and a face flushed from sunshine or booze – possibly both. He was still in his twenties, but his dour expression and a couple of scars made him seem older.

'Hi, Sarge,' he said. 'We're trying to open these wells.'

'What do you mean by *trying*?'

'The problem is that in blowing the concrete apart, we might also destroy the walls, covering the concrete with more debris and fucking the wells up for good.'

'Which means we fuck up the village for good.'

'Yes, boss, that's it.'

Lampton glanced at the well behind the man, his attention drawn by what sounded like the tapping of a hammer coming up from its depths. 'What are the chances of success?'

'Pretty good,' the man said, 'but not guaranteed. It's a calculated gamble, I guess, but I've orders to try it.'

'Why not?' Lampton said, glancing at the villagers gathered together across the clearing, though being kept a safe distance away by some troopers. 'If it fails, those poor sods won't have lost any more than they've lost already. This village is dead as we stand here. We can't kill it off more.'

When the red-haired man's sharp blue gaze focused on Ricketts and the other two, Lampton introduced them, then said: 'This is Corporal Alfie Lloyd, formerly a Royal Engineer sapper, then ammunition technician with the Royal Army Ordnance Corps, now an SAS demolition specialist.' He turned back to Lloyd. 'So how's it going, Alfie?'

'Fine, boss. We're all set to go. The wet concrete was originally poured in from mechanical mixers and hardened at the bottom of the walls. We think it's about six foot deep. We've drilled about halfway through it and filled the hole with C3 plastic explosive. There's a man down each well right now, fixing the time fuse, blasting cap and det cord.' He indicated the coils of detonating cord resting on the ground by each well, with one end looped over the wall and snaking down to the bottom, where the sapper below would now be fixing it to the blasting cap. 'We're hoping that with just the right amount of explosive we can shatter the slab concrete without doing damage to the walls around it. If we're successful, the pieces of broken concrete can be hauled up from the bottom of the well in buckets, giving access to the water still below.'

Lloyd turned away from Lampton as the men who had been at the bottom of the wells clambered back over the sides, their bodies criss-crossed with webbing that held explosives, blasting caps and various tools, including wire-clippers and a small, light hammer. When they were completely over the walls, their companions pulled up the rope ladders.

'OK?' Lloyd asked. Both men put their thumbs up. 'Right. Run the other ends of those det cords across to the detonators and let's get this show on the road.' He turned back to Lampton. 'I'd stand over there, if I was you, a safe distance away. About the same distance as those gawking Arabs, in case we've miscalculated.'

'Now you wouldn't do that, would you, Corporal Lloyd?'

'It's best not to take chances.'

'*I'm* not taking any chances,' Gumboot said. 'When I was in Northern Ireland, doing a tour in bandit country, we were called to the scene where some IRA wally had blown himself up by accident when planting a bomb. They gave us plastic rubbish bags and told us to pick up the pieces, which were scattered all over the fucking place. You couldn't tell his dick from his fingers. That put me off explosives for life, so just tell me where to stand.'

'Over there by those houses. Beside the Arabs. Where you belong, mate.'

Clearly knowing that Lloyd had no sense of humour whatsoever, Lampton led the others back across the clearing, until they were level with the detonators on either side of them. As they waited for the sappers to move their demolition gear away from the wells and fix the detonating cords to the detonators, Ricketts asked: 'Were those wells sealed by the SAF?'

'Correct,' Lampton replied. 'As I said, the *adoo* are fanatical communists. About sixteen months ago, just before the old Sultan was deposed by his son, Qaboos, he was informed that this village was sympathetic to the *adoo*, who were then in control of much of the region.

Reacting as he always did, the Sultan sent his SAF troops in to hang the suspected *adoo* and seal the wells, the lifeblood of the village, by pouring in gallons of wet cement direct from mixers. But this didn't stop the *adoo* from carrying out their customary brutalities against the same unfortunate Muslims. They came into the village that very afternoon, while some of the Sultan's victims were still dangling from ropes – deliberately kept up there as a grim reminder to the villagers, and guarded by SAF troops. The *adoo* shot the troops, then engaged in their usual practice of trying to persuade the village elders to publicly renounce Islam. As is one of the *adoo* customs, when the elders refused, their eyes were gouged out and their daughters repeatedly raped. When the *adoo* then melted back into the wadis of the Jebel, the villagers were left without their life-giving water and, even worse, with many of their menfolk dead or blinded. In short, the village was doomed.'

Lampton stopped for a moment to watch the sappers fix the detonating cords to the detonators under the eagle eye of the dour corporal.

'What a fucking awful story!' Gumboot said to Ricketts and Andrew. 'First you get it from one side, then from the other – just like the protection gangs in Northern Ireland.'

'Oh, yeah?' said Andrew. 'What did they do?'

'A bunch of fucking gangsters masquerading as freedom fighters,' Gumboot said. 'First, a Protestant gang would visit a shop and demand payment for so-called protection against the Catholics. If the shopkeeper refused, they either wrecked his shop or burned it down completely. If he accepted, he'd then receive a visit from a Catholic gang demanding payment for so-called protection against the Prods. If he refused, they did the same as the Prods – turned his shop over. If he agreed, the Prods came back and burned the shop down to keep the money from going to the Catholics. The poor fuckers didn't know which way to turn. Often it was just a matter of who got to them first. Just like this place!'

'Religion and politics,' Andrew intoned in a mock-solemn voice, 'are excuses for many evil deeds. Personally, I wash my hands of both and stick to my poetry.'

'Look at those mad fuckers,' Gumboot said, indicating with a nod the sappers, who were kneeling on the ground by the detonators, a hundred yards from the wells, fixing the end of the detonating cords to the charge terminals. 'Did you see that Corporal Lloyd? He had a broken nose and scars on his face and we all know what from – his own fucking explosives. Some job to have, eh?'

'Rather him than me,' Ricketts said.

Satisfied that the sappers were getting on with their business, Lampton turned back to his probationers and continued: 'What was I saying? Ah, yes, the village was doomed ... Well, that's why we're here. Now that this area is back in Sultan Qaboos's hands, it's our job to rescue formerly doomed villages like this, righting the wrongs of the previous Sultan in the name of his son and reminding the Muslims what will happen to them should they let the *adoo* return. In this case, our first task is to open up those wells and give water, therefore life, back to the villagers. Once that's done, we'll bring in some BATT teams, including medics and veterinarians, to restore the sick to health and help the rest get the most out of the water, the crops it'll bring back, and the livestock it'll help to increase. After that, we'll bring in English teachers, radio sets tuned to Radio Salalah, comics, books and other seductive Western luxuries.'

'Propaganda,' Andrew murmured.

'No, Trooper. Hearts and minds.'

'Ain't no one gettin' *my* mind,' Andrew insisted. 'That's all my own, man.'

'With a mind like yours,' Gumboot said, 'no one would want it. You've no cause for concern there.'

'We've already got it,' Lampton said. 'The trooper just doesn't know it yet.'

After grinning at the doubtful Andrew, Lampton returned his gaze to the sappers who were still kneeling on the ground, one at each detonating plunger. The grim-faced Corporal Lloyd checked that the gawking villagers, particularly the children, were being held back by the troopers, then, without ceremony, he told his men to set off the explosive charges. They pressed down simultaneously on the plungers.

At first, the explosions at the bottom of the two wells were muffled by the solid concrete and sheer depth, but as the concrete exploded, the noise became louder, like the roaring of a buried beast. Suddenly, with an even louder roar, the mouths of the two wells spewed clouds of dust, smoke, pulverized concrete — and finally, water.

The villagers erupted into cheers and cries of joy as the water showered up in the air, then rained back down on them, mixed with dust and powdered concrete. When it had settled down and the smoke and dust had cleared away, both villagers and BATT men rushed to the wells to fight for a position around the walls to look down into the depths.

In both wells the slab concrete had been shattered by the explosions and was piled up as rubble at the bottom. But the rubble was loose and easy to haul up, and soon water was clearly visible below. The village was saved.

6

Any doubts that Ricketts and his two friends might have been harbouring about the reality of *adoo* raids were brutally laid to rest on the final day of their five-day tour. Awakened, as usual, at the crack of dawn, which was just after five o'clock; they rolled off their camp-beds, shocked themselves awake with a quick shower and then returned to the bivouac tent to get dressed.

'What the fuck do we have to get up so early for, anyway?' Bill asked, 'when we're not even on patrol, but just farting about the area, getting lessons in diplomacy and other shit from BATT teams?'

'We have to get up at five in the morning,' Andrew told him, 'because whether or not we appreciate the lessons, our wonderful tour guides, such as Sergeant Lampton, like to fill in every minute of the day, from dawn to dusk.'

'He's a damned good guide, though,' Ricketts

said, slipping into his shorts. 'And a nice bloke as well.'

'You only think that,' Gumboot teased, 'because he put you in charge of us.'

'Go fuck yourself, Gumboot.'

'I agree with Ricketts,' Andrew said. 'Lampton's A1. What's your sergeant like, lads?

'OK,' Jock said. 'Like yours, he never gives us a free minute, but otherwise he's not bad. Good-humoured. Pretty relaxed. No problems there.'

'Fuck the sergeants,' Tom said. 'What's weird to me is the fact that having gone through the hell of Initial Selection and Continuation Training, we're not even allowed to wear our berets, let alone any other insignia. I sometimes think I never really did all that – never really got badged.'

'If you hadn't been badged, you wouldn't be here,' Andrew said, 'so get a grip on yourself. Think positive, man!'

While the men got dressed, the radio beside Tom's camp-bed informed them that the official IRA had condemned a recent pub bombing by the Provisionals in which two people had been killed; that 32 inmates and ten wardens had died in a prison riot at the Attica State Correction Facility in New York state; and that Chelsea had beaten Jeunesse Hautcharage 13–0 in the second round of the European Cup Winners

Cup. The news was followed by the ravings of a demented DJ introducing Rod Stewart's hit, *Maggie May*.

Tom switched the radio off when they all left the bivouac tent, but Gumboot and Bill were singing *Maggie May* as they crossed the dusty clearing to the open mess tent. Inside, they joined the queue to the servery, where they engaged in a little waken-up bullshit with the cook. He had weary eyes and sweat on his vest.

'What's that?' Andrew asked, pointing to the heaped, steaming baked beans. 'Have you been robbing the bog again?'

'You don't like it, Trooper, go climb a tree and pick the kind of grub you're used to.'

'That still leaves us,' Gumboot said, 'and we're in need of some decent grub, though that isn't exactly what I see here. Is that compo sausage or stewed cock?'

'If it's the latter, I'm sure you've tasted it before, so why not try it again?'

'He's just insulted your manhood, Gumboot.'

'He's not a man if he stoops to that. Hey, chef, is that bacon you're putting on my plate or just one of your old shoes?'

'It's tongue,' the cook replied wearily as he slapped the bacon down on Gumboot's plate between the sausage and baked beans. 'It was torn from the throat of the fucker who insulted me yesterday. Now move along, Trooper.'

'A nice man,' Gumboot said, moving along to the tea urn. 'I'm told he washes his hands once a week – when he has his day off.'

Andrew studied his mug of tea. 'A strange colour, folks. It also has an odd smell. Has anyone ever seen that cook in the ablutions or does he piss somewhere else?'

'Smells familiar,' Ricketts said.

'Pungent,' Andrew clarified.

'Close your eyes and think of England,' Gumboot said, 'when you have to swallow the stuff.'

'Hey, you bunch,' the cook bawled, glaring at them, 'you're holding up the whole queue. Clear off to the tables.'

'Yes, mother!' Andrew piped.

They sat around one of the trestle tables near the open end of the tent, from where they could see the rest of Um al Gwarif, including the other SAS tents, the whitewashed Wali's fort, the SAF barracks, and the officers' mess and accommodations partially hidden behind a row of palm trees. When a 25-pounder roared from beyond the perimeter, they all looked automatically in that direction, actually seeing the shell leave the smoking barrel. A few seconds later, a column of smoke and dust billowed up where the shell exploded on the lower slopes of the Jebel.

'I'm amazed there's any *adoo* left up there at all,' Tom said, holding a fork heaped with baked beans to his mouth. 'Those 25-pounders fire on the Jebel every couple of hours, day in and day out. It must be sheer hell up there.'

'They rarely hit anything,' Ricketts said as Tom swallowed his baked beans. 'Or if they do, it's just by accident. They're just firing at random to keep the *adoo* on their toes and preferably sleepless.'

'That's why we're all so exhausted,' Bill put in. '*We're* the ones kept awake!'

As the sand and dust thrown up by the big gun drifted back down over the hedgehog, slightly obscuring the view of the plateau, an unshaven white man wearing a filthy striped jellaba and loose *shemagh* stopped at the adjoining, empty table. He had an L42A1 7.62mm bolt-action Lee Enfield sniper rifle slung across his back and his webbing bristled with ten-round box magazines and L2A2 steel-cased fragmentation grenades. There was a Browning high-power handgun in a holster on his hip and two different knives – the fearsome Omani *kunjias* and a Fairburn-Sykes commando knife – were sheathed on the belt around his waist. Sitting down at the table next to them, neither smiling nor talking to anyone, he placed his plate of compo on the table, then unslung his rifle and aimed it at the smoke still boiling up from the lower slopes of the Jebel. He pretended to fire, making a clicking sound with his tongue. Then, still not smiling, he placed his rifle on the table beside his plate and began to eat.

Tom leaned sideways and whispered to his best friend, Bill: 'That's Sergeant Parker! They all talk about him. They say he's the best sniper and tracker in the whole SAS.'

'Looks pretty fierce,' Bill said.

'Apparently he is. Dresses up in those old Arab clothes and goes out there on a camel, criss-crossing the whole plateau, sniping on the *adoo* and often bringing prisoners back for questioning. He's waging a private war out there and causing a lot of confusion.'

'Glad he's on our side,' Bill said. 'Wouldn't want him against me.'

'Apparently he's going to be with us when we make the assault on the Jebel. They say he now knows as much about the Jebel as any tribesman.'

'He *looks* like one,' Bill said. 'As mad and as bad. Well . . .' he sighed melodramatically, 'nice to know we're protected.'

Hearing what they had just said, Andrew

turned towards the man dressed like an Arab and said with a big smile, 'Hi, there, Sarge!'

Parker stopped eating just long enough to turn his head and stare at Andrew with the steady, fathomless gaze of a cat. He did not say a word.

Glancing briefly at the others, Andrew cleared his throat, kept his smile firmly in place and turned back to Parker.

'How are things up on the Jebel, then?' he asked. 'Pretty hot up there – right, boss?'

Parker just stared at him as if at a blank wall, his fork still raised in the air, with an untouched piece of sausage on it.

Andrew cleared his throat again. 'Still picking off the *adoo*, are you? Still bringing them back down the hill for a talk with the green slime? Good work, Sarge. Keep it up!'

Parker just stared at him, his gaze as firm as it was unreadable, then opened his mouth and popped the sausage in, turning back to his plate. Andrew, clearing his throat for the third time, pushed his chair back and stood up. 'Well,' he said, louder than strictly necessary, 'I think it's time we all left, lads. Lots to do out on the Salalah plain. A long day ahead of us.' He was out of the tent before Ricketts and Gumboot had kicked their own chairs back, but they soon caught up with him. 'Did you see the way he looked at me?' he said. 'With those mad-dog eyes! A born killer if ever I saw one. I'm still shaking, man!'

'You imagined it,' Ricketts said consolingly. 'You're a poet – imaginative. It was all in your head. He's just the quiet type, that's all.'

Andrew shook his head from side to side, clearly not convinced. 'No, man, I didn't imagine a thing – that was one real mean mother. He's the kind to use barbed wire as dental floss, and wipe his arse with sandpaper. You say the wrong thing to him, man, and you'll end up as mince-meat on his plate. Hey, I'm still sweatin' and shakin'. Let's go find Sergeant Lampton and get out of here. I need the wide, open spaces.'

'Yes, let's do that,' Ricketts said, glancing sideways and grinning at Gumboot. 'It's time to start anyway.'

Walking the short distance to the motor pool, they found Sergeant Lampton waiting in the Land Rover, pressed back in the front passenger seat with his knees bent and his desert boots on the dash board, smoking. He made a show of looking at his wristwatch when they approached him.

'You were nearly late,' he said.

'Sorry, boss,' Ricketts replied. 'Trooper Winston became involved in conversation with a sergeant named Parker.'

'Dead-eye Dick,' Lampton replied.

'Pardon?'

Lampton slid his feet off the dashboard and sat up straight. 'Dead-eye Dick. That's what they call him. He's probably the best sniper in Oman – and he's quick with those knives, as well. You mean, he actually *spoke* to you?'

'Well, not exactly . . .' Andrew began.

'It was kind of one-sided,' Ricketts explained, 'but Andrew was certainly trying.'

Ricketts, Gumboot and Lampton all burst out laughing.

'Very funny,' Andrew said, heaving his great bulk into the back of the Land Rover.

'*Very* funny!' Gumboot said. 'Fucking had me in stitches!'

'I'll have you in stitches in a minute if you don't shut your mouth.'

'OK, lads, cool it.' Lampton flicked his cigarette butt out of the vehicle. 'We'll start the day with a morning visit to the BATT house at Rakyut, which is somewhere you haven't been before. OK, Ricketts, let's go.'

'Yes, boss.' Ricketts released the handbrake, slipped into gear, pressed his foot on the accelerator and drove towards the main gate. Just before he reached it, there was an explosion from beyond the perimeter, followed by a billowing cloud of smoke.

The sirens on the watch-towers started wailing. Ricketts braked to a halt as two RAF guards sprinted out of the sangars on either side of the main gate, intending to close it.

'Leave it open!' Lampton bawled. 'We're going out!'

As the guards stopped to stare in surprise at Lampton, he turned to Ricketts, slapped his shoulder and shouted, 'Go, damn it!' Ricketts put his foot right down and raced out through the gate, turning in the direction of the boiling cloud of smoke, even as the RAF guards closed the gate and sprinted back to their sangars.

By now the machine-guns in the watch-towers to the front of the camp had started roaring, sending steams of purplish tracers looping over the billowing cloud of black smoke and exploding in the ground further on.

'Bloody *adoo*!' Lampton exclaimed, glancing to where earth and sand was spewing up from the impact of the 7.62mm GPMG shells.

Straight ahead, just beside the dirt track, the Saladin armoured car used for the daily sweep of the terrain was lying on its side, pouring black smoke. A scorched, horribly blistered figure was crawling from the wreckage. Just as Ricketts was accelerating towards him, however, another figure, wearing loose pants, sandals and a *shemagh*, emerged from behind some rocks, darted up to the crawling figure, and drove a *kunjias* through the back of his neck. After grabbing the dead man's wristwatch, pistol and spare ammunition, the Arab hurried back behind the nearby rocks.

'Bastard!' While Ricketts was still driving, Lampton pulled out his Browning handgun and fired a short burst at the fleeing man. Pieces of stone flew off the rocks in clouds of spewing dust, but the Arab disappeared, untouched. Then a fusillade of fire from behind the rocks made Ricketts swerve off the track and brake to a halt beside the smouldering armoured car, which offered protection.

It also offered a grisly view of the RAF guards inside, all dead, either slashed to pieces by flying, red-hot metal or burned alive in the flaming vehicle.

'Shit!' Lampton jumped out of the Land Rover. He was followed by Ricketts, Andrew and Gumboot, who took up positions on either side of the smoking vehicle. Stifling their urge to throw up at the smell of burning flesh, they poured a hail of SLR fire at the mound of rocks, where they assumed the *adoo* assassin was still hiding.

No more gunfire came from behind the rocks, but Lampton still made no move. Only when the tracers from the watch-tower started falling farther away, indicating that the *adoo* were beating a retreat, did he take a chance by racing around the overturned armoured car and heading straight for the mound of rocks.

Ricketts and the other two gave him covering fire until he reached where he was going. He fired a burst behind the rocks, stepped forward, glanced down, then raised his right hand, waving it to and fro, indicating 'Cease fire'. The guns on the watch-towers then fell silent.

Lampton walked back to the blazing armoured car. He glanced with distaste at the dead men inside. The other victim was lying face-down on the ground with the back of his neck pumping blood. Turning the latter on his back, Lampton checked that he was dead, then shook his head.

'Didn't have a prayer,' he said. He glanced back at the mound of rocks from which the *adoo* had been firing. 'And those bastards,' he said. 'The invisible men. They've gone already – all of them – clean away.'

Returning to the Land Rover, he called base on the PRC 319, explaining what had happened and asking them to send out an ambulance and tow truck with crew. Both arrived within minutes, the former to remove the dead bodies, the latter to put out the fire on the overturned armoured car, hoist it the right way up, then transport it back to the wrecker's yard.

Lampton and the others followed in the Land Rover, now destined to spend the rest of the morning in camp, submitting a report of the grim event.

7

Every evening, being covered in a slimy film of dust and sweat, the newcomers trooped off for a cleansing, cooling shower. This was followed by 'prayers', a meeting of personnel where the ops captain would read out the day's news about Dhofar and then a summary of world news. Failure to attend the meeting without good cause led to the standard SAS punishment of a fine. 'Prayers' was followed by dinner in the open-sided mess tent. Then the evening was free. It was spent either in the NAAFI tent, running up a tab with Pete, or at the outdoor cinema, where, on alternate nights, they could watch the latest English or American movies, supplied by the Service Kinema Corporation. The men invariably went straight back to the NAAFI tent after the movie, where they would help themselves to more Tiger beer from the fridge and discuss the film with Pete, the movie buff.

'Close to the fucking bone,' Gumboot said.

'Humping there in the grass in the winter with overcoats on. No wonder Mary Whitehouse and Lord Longford are all up in arms.'

'Well, it *was* called *Carnal Knowledge*,' Andrew reminded him, 'so what *else* could they show?'

'I think the idea was to satirize it,' Pete explained, 'which Mike Nichols did well.'

'It wasn't Mike Nichols,' Bill said, looking a little confused. 'It was that other guy — what's-his-name? Jack *Nicholson*. The one with the leer.'

'Mike Nichols is the director, you stupid prat.'

'Sorry, Pete.'

'That Ann-Margret was gorgeous,' Ricketts said.

'A good actress, too,' Pete pointed out.

'Yeah,' Jock chimed in. 'You could tell that by the size of her knockers. She should get an award.'

'She did,' Pete the Buff said. 'Academy nomination.'

'I saw her in that *Viva Las Vegas*,' Gumboot said, 'with good old hound dog, Elvis Presley. Boy, can that guy sing!'

'I saw that film as well,' Andrew said. 'Ann-Margret walked away with the picture. Christ, she was sexy!'

'She displayed more of her talents in *Carnal*

Knowledge,' Tom said, trying to be as witty as Jock. 'Those enormous, bare boobs!'

'What a bunch of bloody philistines,' Pete said, puffing his pipe and opening another bottle of Tiger. 'It's like talking to Neanderthal men. Where do you guys get off?'

'On Ann-Margret,' Andrew said.

Invariably, during the movies, the nearby 'hedgehogs', picking up a reading of ground movement on their Battlefield Surveillance (ZB) radar, would let rip with 81mm mortars and 7.62mm GPMGs, webbing the starry night beyond the big outdoor screen with tracer fire. This encouraged incoming green tracer from the defiant adoo. Though the noise and spectacular *son et lumière* shows were something of a distraction, they did not actually interrupt the films.

'Shut that racket!' some men bawled.

'Fucking gunners!' cried out others.

'Those guns went off just as Ann-Margret came,' Andrew observed. 'I think that's symbolic.'

As they had only been on the base five days and nights, and as Indian-language films were shown on alternate nights, the new arrivals only managed to see two English-language movies. The second was *Kelly's Heroes*, starring Clint Eastwood.

'Now there's *my* man,' Gumboot said. 'A real actor, old Clint. He's supposed to be as good a shot in real life as he is in the movies. Bloody marvellous, he is!'

'Disappointing in that one, though.' Pete was drunk and thoughtful as he stoked his smouldering pipe. 'I prefer him in those great spaghetti westerns as the Man from Nowhere.'

'Load of shite, that film was.' Jock was on his fourth bottle. 'I mean *Kelly's Heroes*. A straight steal from *The Dirty Dozen*. Did you ever see soldiers behaving that way? Not on your nelly!'

'Yeah, right,' Bill said, smoking a cigarette and sipping his Tiger. 'We're supposed to believe that a bunch of World War Two GIs could march into a German-occupied town and rob the bloody bank. What a load of dog's balls!'

'Not to mention Donald Sutherland,' Tom added. 'They're always casting him as a soldier, yet he walks and talks like the living dead. He didn't convince me a bit.'

'Right,' Gumboot said 'I can't imagine *him* doing Sickener One, let alone Sickener Two.'

'I can't imagine *you* doing them,' Andrew said, 'but you somehow got through.'

'Oh, very funny, Trooper Winston. I can't imagine how they let *you* through the course and gave you a badge.'

'It's 'cause they thought I was pretty. Also, I'm as tough as nails, as brave as a lion, and one of the best soldiers in the Regiment. What more can I say?'

'Don't say anything, Andrew. Just let us see what you're like when we tackle the Jebel. You'll be pissing in your pants, shitting bricks, so don't come it with me, mate!'

Big Andrew grinned at him. 'Oh, I'm not worried. I know you'll be right there by my side, my protector and hero. I feel so lucky, Gumboot.'

Noting that Andrew had mockingly lisped the final sentence, Gumboot shook his head in disgust. 'What a ponce!' he said.

But, for all their joking, few of them had forgotten the one subject they rarely discussed – the forthcoming assault on the Jebel Dhofar. Few of them could forget it because it was always there before them, soaring up to the sky and dominating the landscape no matter in which direction they drove across the Salalah plain. From there, at ground level, the plateau looked enormous, too high to be climbed; it was also strewn with wadis which were, as they knew, filled with hundreds of *adoo*, most of them crack marksmen and fanatics only too willing to die for their cause. As Major Greenaway had pointed out, the *adoo* would be a formidable enemy. Also formidable would be the Jebel itself, though they rarely discussed this fact.

On the sixth morning, the day after the armoured car had been ambushed, they were driven out of the base for a few more days of weapons training in the boiling heat and dust of the Arzat ranges. Regardless of the heat, they were kept at it all day every day, practising on the firing range and learning to clean and reassemble their weapons in the harsh, unwelcoming desert.

It was hell on the firing range, the heat relentless, the light too bright, and the dust got up their nostrils and filled their mouths, clogging chambers and barrels and jamming the works. The ground did not really belong to human beings, but to poisonous scorpions and centipedes, as well as hideous camel spiders, while the very air they breathed was filled with fat, buzzing flies, whining mosquitoes and stinging hornets, all of which had to be constantly swatted away while the men were trying to take aim and fire.

'This is useless,' Jock groaned. 'I can't even take aim. Every time I try to squint through the sight, I get sand or dust or some other shit in my eye. As for breathing – forget it. You'll only swallow a fucking hornet. And each time I squeeze the trigger, I get bit by a mosquito, so I jerk and go a mile off the target. I say call it a day.'

'I say keep your trap shut, Trooper,' their instructor, Sergeant Bannerman, said, 'and try to put a bullet in that target instead of moaning and groaning. Annoy me and you'll cop an RTU and find yourself on a plane back to England before you can blink . . . Hey, you! That's right, the big black one! What the hell are you doing?'

'Pardon, boss?' Andrew asked. Having just yelped and rolled frantically to the side, he was looking up at Bannerman with wide, shocked eyes.

'What the hell do you think you're doing, Trooper, wriggling and yelping there like a woman getting a good piece?'

'Bloody spider, boss. A great big hairy thing! It had a body the size of my hand and 'orrible little legs.'

'So?'

'*What*, boss?'

'It's a spider – so what? It wasn't a fucking scorpion or centipede, so what the hell are you worried about? Get back on your belly!'

'But it's still there, boss! Right in front of where I'm lying. It's looking me right in the eye and it gives me the shivers.'

Gumboot sniggered. Bannerman glared at him. 'You think this is funny, Trooper? A big joke to you, is it? If it's so bloody funny, why not go over there and pick up that perfectly harmless camel spider and bring it to me?'

'Er . . .' Gumboot stuttered.

'Go on,' Andrew said, suddenly feeling a lot better at getting his own back, 'let's see you do it.'

'Who gives the orders around here, Trooper?'

'Pardon, boss?' Andrew asked.

'I give the orders around here, Trooper, and don't you forget it. Now roll back on your belly and ignore that bloody spider and put a bullet into the target before I put one in you.'

'Yes, sir!'

Luckily, when Andrew did as he was told, the spider was gone. But the incident, as well as providing some mirth, was a reminder of just how antagonistic the desert was, even here on the firing range, and of what they could expect to find when they started climbing the Jebel. It merely made the firing range more hateful and increased their other concerns about what was to come.

As the *adoo* were renowned marksmen who could chalk up kills from a great distance while remaining well hidden, the troopers were issued, apart from their customary 30-round M16s, with a range of sniper rifles, including the L42A1 7.62mm Lee Enfield bolt-action and the L1A1 SLR semi-automatic. These, in the furnace of the firing range, they were required to repeatedly disassemble, clean of dust and sand, oil, and reassemble – sometimes blindfolded.

However, as the likelihood of close contact with the *adoo* was likely, they were also issued with Heckler & Koch MP5 9mm sub-machine-guns, or SMGs, and practised firing them from the sitting, kneeling and standing positions in single shots, three-round bursts, and on fully automatic, using 30-round magazines at a rate of 800rpm. They were also trained in the MP5K, a shorter version of the MP5, with a 15-round magazine, and used as a semi-automatic replacement for the pistol; and in the MP5SD, also a short-barrelled model, but including a visual sight with a tell-tale red dot indicating the mean point of impact, or MPI.

More ominous was the instructors' insistence that they endlessly practice the various methods of firing their standard-issue Browning 9mm high-power handguns. The fact that this insistence was combined with the sudden appearance of the Heckler & Koch MP5 range of SMGs – which were, in effect, automatic pistols – only made the men realize that the Head Sheds, their senior officers, were anticipating more than ordinarily close contact with the enemy – possibly even hand-to-hand fighting.

Be that as it may, they were retrained in the

Hereford lessons for the Browning: the one-handed, two-handed and alert positions; standing, kneeling and prone; breathing, squeeze, and release-trigger hand pressure; adjusting the aim in the midst of firing. These lessons, too, were carried out in the blazing sun, amid the dust and the flies and other insects.

The fact that a couple of the men collapsed in the heat during this retraining did nothing to deter their instructors, who pointed out that they would have to endure similar, and possibly worse, conditions during the assault on the Jebel. Indeed, for this very reason, even while the remaining men were boiling in the heat and choking in the dust, they were severely restricted in their use of water, this being their instructors' way of teaching them to discipline themselves against chronic thirst for long periods of time.

As they sat 'resting' between firing lessons or drills – which in fact meant being tortured further by the heat and dust – they were forced to listen to lectures on ways of combating dehydration, sunstroke, sunburn and, of course, lack of water. Naturally, while listening to such lectures, some of the men started suffering from dehydration, others came close to sunstroke and sunburn, and all of them nearly went mad with the need for a drink.

'It'll be easier up on the plateau,' Andrew gasped, when finally they were allowed to sip some water. 'Nothing on earth could be worse than this.'

'I wouldn't bet on it,' Lampton said.

While in Arzat, they slept at night on the ground, shocked by how cold it was after the day's scorching heat. Yet even in the cold they had to shake out their kit, invariably finding scorpions, centipedes or camel spiders in at least one or two of the canvas sheets. And, though it was cold, the night was still filled with whining mosquitoes, dive-bombing hornets, flying beetles, and bloated flies, none of which ever seemed to sleep, all ravenous for human sweat and blood. The nights were therefore filled with the sounds of muttered curses and hands slapping bare skin.

'I'm amazed I've any blood left at all,' Gumboot said, examining the ugly mosquito bites all over his arms and legs.

'I sympathize,' Andrew said. He had decided to be nice to Gumboot. 'You look like a bloody pincushion and you never stop scratching. Maybe it's syphilis.'

'Ha, ha, very funny,' Gumboot said, still scratching compulsively.

Though an experienced regular soldier, Ricketts also found himself unable to sleep, not only because of the constantly diving, whining hornets and mosquitoes, but also because of persistent thoughts of the attack on the armoured car and the savagery with which the RAF guards had been killed. He was particularly haunted by the recollection of the *adoo* soldier driving the long blade of his *kunjias* through the back of the neck of the burnt man crawling face-down on the ground. The man had made no sound, which suggested that the long blade had gone right through his neck to his throat and vocal cords, but his body had jumped and quivered hideously as the blood gushed out of his neck and splashed over the Arab. That recollection, more than anything else, seemed nightmarish to Ricketts.

Then there was the mountain, the Jebel Dhofar, looming over him even now, where he lay on the hard ground, using his bergen as a pillow, hoping that the cream smeared on his skin would keep the insects and creepy-crawlies away, particularly those with venomous stings, such as the scorpion and centipede. The Jebel was dark now, even darker than the night, and given shape only by the stars that appeared to fall all around it. It was dark, immense, very high, and unknown, probably mined and filled with the *adoo*, who were practically part of it.

Ricketts, though exhausted and full of aches

and pains, wanting to sleep and unable to do so, looked to the mountain with an odd, unfamiliar mixture of fear and excitement. He wanted to brave the very thing that frightened him and thus blow it away. That's what made him a trooper.

Returning to the base at Um al Gwarif, sun-tanned, covered in filth, badly bitten, sleepless, with eyes sore from constantly squinting into the sun, the men were only given time for a quick shower and meal, then ordered to the 'hotel' for a briefing about the assault on the Jebel, due to take place the next day.

Once in the big marquee, they were split into teams and sat around a couple of standard British Army six-foot tables with their individual maps of Dhofar spread out in front of them. The Intelligence Corps officer arrived shortly after, shook the hand of B Squadron's commander, Major Greenaway, and was then introduced as Captain Butler. A larger map of Dhofar was pinned to a board behind the table with the words 'OPERATION JAGUAR – SECRET' stencilled across the top of it.

'Tomorrow's operation,' Butler began, 'code-named Jaguar, has been designed to secure us our first firm base on the enemy-held Jebel around the village of Jibjat. The starting point is a former

Sultan's Air Force base on the plain known as Lympne. The mixed assault force, consisting of SAS, SAF and *firqats*, will total 800 men. It will be split into two. The majority of B Squadron and G Squadron 22 SAS, the Firqat Al Asifat, the Firqat Salahadeen, and the Baluch Askars are tasked to assault the airfield at Lympne on foot. The remainder of the force will be choppered in after a firm base has been established.'

Using a pointer to show the various locations, Butler continued: 'At first light we'll leave the SAF staging post of Midway, located north of the Negd plain. From there, we'll drive south-east until we reach the foothills of the Jebel and the entrance to this major wadi.' He pointed to the beginning of the Jebel. 'We'll follow the wadi bottom until we run out of motorable track. We'll then debus and move on foot to an area known as the Mahazair Pools, where already we have a small base camp. As the monsoon's just finished, there should be plenty of water there, which is why we're making it our rest area.'

As if to remind them all that the *adoo* were still up there on the Jebel, waiting for them, the 25-pounders boomed from just outside the perimeter. A lot of the men glanced at one another, some grinning nervously.

'The actual operation against the airfield will be mounted the following night,' Butler continued. 'The climb into the hills will be exhausting. Almost certainly it will also involve a running battle with the *adoo*. We will, however, have resups from the Skyvans and air support from the Strikemasters. No matter how difficult, we must keep advancing until we reach the rough airstrips and the few watering-holes on the high plain. That's where most of the *adoo* are entrenched. Our task is to get them out for good and take command of the area. If we succeed, we'll deal a serious blow to their morale and gain the support of most of the local populace.'

Captain Butler put the pointer down and faced the men again. 'Any questions?'

'What kind of resistance is expected, boss?' Tom Purvis asked.

'Regarding the makeshift airfield at Lympne, we're anticipating that a diversionary attack to the south will draw the *adoo* away long enough for our main assault force to encircle the area without resistance. Once the *adoo* return, a battle lasting weeks, or even months, is the least we expect. It won't be an easy battle, as the *adoo* are heavily armed with state-of-the-art Soviet and Chinese automatic weapons, including Kalashnikov AK-47s, Simonev semi-automatics, RPG 7s, RPD light machine-guns, GPMGs and 82mm mortars. The battle, however, no matter how brutal and lengthy, will be followed by the surrender of the *adoo* before the next monsoon season, beginning in June. Nobody has ever stayed on the Jebel through the monsoon, so it should be over by then. Any *more* questions?'

'Did you say *months*, boss?' Bill Raglan asked.

'You heard me, Trooper.'

'No more questions, boss.'

The men left the 'hotel' to prepare their kit, a task which took up most of the remainder of the evening. This done, they shook out the sheets on their camp-beds, checking for scorpions and centipedes, then tried to catch the last remotely decent sleep they would have for a long time.

They were up again at the crack of dawn.

8

The men did not set out at the crack of dawn. Instead, after they had dressed in their OGs and jungle hats, they had a long morning of personal kit and weapons inspection, conducted by Sergeant Lampton and RSM Worthington, both of whom displayed a ruthless talent for spotting even the slightest speck of dirt or sand in the weapons, a loose strap or damaged webbing. More than one man was sent on the double to the armoury or the Quartermaster's stores to replace faulty parts or damaged items, returning shamefaced to his bivouac for another bollocking from the redoubtable RSM.

Nor did it end there. Once the kit inspections were over, the men were marched to the firing range, where every personal weapon was checked by actually being fired. Nevertheless, by lunchtime, the troop was ready to move and the men were allowed a last visit to the NAAFI tent for a decent lunch.

'Mutton curry!' Bill groaned. 'I don't bloody believe it! We're going to be on the march for days and they serve up compo *curry*!'

'We'll be shitting our pants as we climb the Jebel,' Gumboot said. 'I call that good planning.'

'The planning's in the rice pudding,' Andrew informed them. 'That stuff will stick like glue to your guts and keep the diarrhoea in. It's kind of an antidote.'

'Five minutes!' the RSM bawled from the open end of the tent. 'Bolt it down and get out of there!'

'Bolting your food down causes indigestion,' Tom complained. 'My dear mother swore to that.'

'Diarrhoea, constipation and indigestion,' Jock said dourly. 'We're in for a right mix.'

They nevertheless obeyed the RSM, bolting down their food and hurrying out of the mess tent to gather together by the Bedfords parked outside the armoury. There, though already heavily burdened with their standard-issue US 5.56mm M16 rifle, 9mm Browning high-power handgun, packed bergen, ammunition pouch, smoke and fragmentation grenades, escape/evasion survival kit and water bottles, they were burdened even more with the selective distribution of L42A1 7.62mm Lee Enfield sniper rifles; two different versions of the Heckler & Koch MP5 9mm sub-machine-gun; the L7A2 general-purpose machine-gun, or GPMG, also known as the 'gimpy'; M-72 LAWs, or Light Anti-Tank Weapons; 51mm mortars with smoke bombs and L16 ML 81mm mortars with base plate, tripod and shells; plus Clansman high-frequency and PRC 319 portable radio systems, with generators and rechargeable batteries.

It took a good half hour to hump the kit into the trucks, but eventually the job was done and the men, having already put in a full day's work, were driven out of Um al Gwarif, across the road, then onto the rough ground beside it, where they shook, rattled and rolled the three miles to RAF Salalah.

After being waved through the main gates by an armed SAF soldier, under the watchful eyes of two RAF guards, the Bedfords parked by the dispersal bays for the Skyvan cargo planes. Corporal Harry Whistler of 55 Air Despatch Squadron, RCT, was there with other pilots and RAF loadmasters, most of them stripped to the waist, gleaming with sweat, and covered in the dust that billowed up from the ground every time they moved a crate of supplies to slide it into the cargo bay in the rear of a Skyvan.

'Are these heaps ready to fly?' Major Greenaway asked Whistler as the rest of the men piled off their individual Bedfords and started sorting out their gear.

'No problem, boss,' Whistler said. 'These supplies will soon be back. The men can start boarding immediately. By the time they're all on board, we'll be ready for take-off.'

'Very good, Corporal.' Greenaway turned to RSM Worthington and told him to divvy the hundred SAS men up and get them on board the half-dozen Skyvans. Even with that number, the pilots would have to make quite a few trips to get the whole complement of men and equipment to the SAF staging post of Midway. Worthington therefore divided them into groups, allocated certain of the groups to individual Skyvans, and told the rest to wait in the minimal shade offered by the walls of oil drums. The latter men let out melodramatic groans of misery.

'Stop whining,' Worthington said. 'To save the Skyvan pilots from having to make too many return trips, the CO's roped in the RAF's three Hueys and the Sikorski light chopper. You men will be going in those.' The four helicopters in the dispersal bays 200 yards away roared into life even as he spoke. Glancing at them, then turning back to Greenaway, Worthington said: 'They're leaving sooner than I thought. What about you, boss?'

'You and I are going in the Sikorski,' Greenaway

said. 'So let's get these men in the Hueys first.'

'Right, boss.' Worthington turned to the troopers who had been moaning and groaning. 'OK, you men, come with us.' The men fell in behind Greenaway and Worthington, following them towards the helicopters as overdone groans came from the men waiting to board the Skyvans.

'OK, lads,' Sergeant Lampton said to Ricketts and the other newcomers, 'we've been lucky. Good old Whistler's going to put us onto his personal Skyvan, so we'll be one of the first groups to take off. Come on, let's go.'

Having assumed that Lampton would be remaining with the BATT teams, Ricketts had been surprised, though pleased, to learn that he was in fact taking part in Operation Jaguar as their platoon leader. Now he was glad to follow him across to Whistler's Skyvan. The RAF corporal was standing by the cargo hold, stripped to the waist as usual, his dark hair falling over his bloodshot eyes, shoulders and arms glistening with sweat, his face red from the sun.

'Hello again!' he said to Ricketts and the others. 'How did your week go?'

'Pretty good,' Ricketts said.

'I hear you had a little trouble at Um al Gwarif.'

'First blood,' Lampton said. 'But they did okay.'

Whistler's grin broadened. 'A taste of what's to come, lads. The *adoo* aren't scared of man or beast – as you'll find out soon enough.' He jerked his thumb back over his shoulder. 'OK, we'll soon be finished here, so get in the plane and take a seat. We'll be taking off in no time.'

'Just don't leave us to fry in there,' Gumboot said, 'with a long wait in this heat.'

'I won't,' Whistler said.

Some of the Skyvans had already roared into life and even as Whistler spoke were taxiing out of the dispersal bays, heading for the runway. At the same time, first one, then two of the American-built Hueys also roared into life, adding their din to that of the aircraft. Suddenly, the whole area had become a hive of activity, with restraining blocks being pulled away from wheels, Skyvan cargo-hold doors being closed, spinning helicopter rotors creating clouds of swirling dust, the Bedfords whining noisily as they reversed and turned away, empty, and line men, or marshallers, with ear defenders driving out in jeeps to the runway to guide the aircraft with hand signals to the holding point on the runway.

Meanwhile, Lampton led his team of probationers into the passenger cabin of the Skyvan, where they strapped themselves into the cramped seats, three to a row, with no aisle down the middle. Ricketts was sitting between Lampton and Andrew.

'Christ,' Andrew complained, 'it's like a furnace in here.'

'Not much space, it's true,' Lampton said, 'but at least the flight will be brief.'

'*How* far is the LZ?' Ricketts asked.

'About fifty-fives miles north of the Jebel.'

'Get me out of this plane and I'll *run* the fifty-five miles,' Andrew said.

Lampton grinned. 'Don't you like planes, Trooper?'

'I hate the bloody things – particularly bathtubs like this. The old Hercules transport isn't so bad, but this . . .' Andrew shrugged. 'Do we flap our arms or what?'

'You just twist the rubber bands and let them go,' Ricketts replied. 'The propellers should spin then.'

'If this thing takes off and lands in one piece, I'll start believing in God.'

'Don't let Whistler hear you saying things like that,' Lampton warned him. 'He's in love with this plane and he'd throw you out without thinking twice.'

'My lips are sealed from this moment on.'

The Skyvan did at least have windows, through

which Ricketts could see the first of the Hueys
taking off, rising vertically, heavily, like the
bloated flies he had seen so often since coming
to Oman. A metallic grinding noise, followed
by loud banging, came from behind him as
the rear cargo-hold door was wound down
and locked. Less than a minute later, Whistler
entered the aircraft by the front door and
disappeared behind the wall dividing the pilot's
cabin from the rest of the plane. The loadmasters,
Ricketts knew, would be sitting in the rear loading bay, communicating with Whistler through
their headphones and mikes. Glancing out the
window, he saw the Sikorski taking off, whipping
up immense clouds of dust, rising towards the last
of the three Hueys, all heading for Midway. At
that moment, the Skyvan's STOL twin engines
roared into life, making the rotors spin, and
the aircraft shuddered violently, then moved
forward, taxiing out of its dispersal bay and
heading for the runway. Within minutes it was
racing along the runway and lifting off, following
the other aircraft and choppers into the brilliant,
blue-white sky above the Salalah plain.

The journey took no time at all, which was
a small mercy, as the interior of the Skyvan
was suffocatingly hot, and they landed at the
SAF staging post of Midway. The disused oil

exploration camp consisted of no more than a number of Twynam huts scattered around an old airstrip in the desolate wasteland of the Negd plain and guarded by SAF troops wearing *shemaghs* and carrying 7.62mm FN rifles. A lot of Bedfords had been already brought in and were lined up along the runway near the huts, where the troops just lifted in by the helicopters were milling about, stretching their legs, smoking, drinking water and making wry jokes.

'Heaven on earth,' Gumboot said sourly, glancing around him, then spitting on the dusty ground at his feet. 'A real home from home.'

'It could be worse,' Andrew replied, mopping the sweat from his face with a handkerchief as the helicopters took off again. 'Just think – you could be back home in Devon, ankle-deep in cow crap and being nagged by your missus. Thank God for small mercies.'

'Well,' Whistler said when his men had unloaded everything from the rear cargo hold and were drawing the door down, 'I'm on my way again, though I guess I'll be coming back with the *firqats*. Best of luck up there, lads.'

'We'll call you if we need you,' Ricketts said, 'so have some Burmail bombs ready.'

Whistler grinned and stuck his thumb up. 'Will do,' he said, then turned away and got back in the Skyvan. As the aircraft was taking off, creating a hell of swirling dust and sand, the men picked up what kit they did not have on them and hurried away from the slipstream. They stopped by the Bedfords at the edge of the runway. The CO and Worthington were near the old huts, shaking hands with the SAF commander, who, like the rest of his men, was wearing a dark-green *shemagh*. Looking in the other direction, Ricketts watched one Skyvan after another take off and disappear into the darkening late-afternoon sky.

'All right, you men, gather round!' Worthington suddenly bawled. 'The CO wants to speak to you.'

When the men had assembled in front of Greenaway, the major said, 'It's going to take all day for the Skyvans and choppers to bring in the remainder of the assault force. We'll therefore be spending the rest of the afternoon and all night here, then move out at first light. In the meantime, you can basha down on that strip of waste ground near the SAF barracks' – he pointed to the dusty old huts – 'and boil up a brew. Don't plan on a rest, as you'll be needed to help with the unloading, which should take half the night. All right, men, that's it.'

When Greenaway and Worthington walked off with the SAF commander, the troopers scattered to find a place on the waste ground to the right of the SAF barracks.

'Fucking typical,' Tom said. 'The A-rabs get the barracks and we get the bloody desert floor.'

'It should be the other way around,' Bill complained. 'I mean, those bastards *come* from the bloody desert.'

'And we don't even get a rest,' Jock added. 'We've been up since dawn and now he says we're gonna work half the night. Bloody cheek, if you ask me.'

'Who's asking?' Andrew asked.

'I mean, unloading!' Jock burst out. 'Why the fuck can't the loadmasters do that and let us get a sleep?'

'It would take too long,' Ricketts said. 'We'd never get it done by dawn. We have to be on our way by first light, so we have to help them unload.'

'Then let the SAF do it instead of hanging around like ponces. I'm amazed they didn't ask us to guard duty as well, to give those SAF sods a rest.'

'On the ground again,' Gumboot said. 'We'll get bitten to death. Every creepy-crawlie known to man and beast is gonna be creeping and crawling over us, after our sweat and blood. Filthy fucking bastards.'

'Poetry and alliteration!' Andrew exclaimed with a wide, mocking smile. 'Hey, Gumboot, you're a real original – pure genius. I'm burning up here with envy.'

'The day you can speak better than me I'll put on a monkey suit. Who fancies a cuppa?'

'Me!' they all cried at once.

Having checked the area for scorpions, centipedes and the like, they put their sleeping bags down and brewed up by boiling water in their mess tins heated on lightweight hexamine stoves.

'Bloody beautiful!' Gumboot said, swiping flies, mosquitoes and hornets from his face and sipping his steaming tea.

The first of the Skyvans arrived back within the hour, when the grey evening light was turning to darkness and the boiling heat was starting to chill. That Skyvan was soon followed by another, then another, all disgorging more supplies and SAF soldiers and *firqats*, the latter looking as fierce as they had done when Ricketts and the other new arrivals had first seen them. Luckily, they were marched off to bed down for the night in another strip of waste ground at the far side of the runway, while the SAF soldiers, of whom the *firqats* did not approve, were given beds or floor space in the SAF barracks.

The extra supplies, of which there were many, kept coming in on plane after plane to be unloaded by the already weary SAS troopers and transported directly to the Bedfords lined up by the runway and guarded by other SAS troops.

'Can't trust those fucking SAF bastards to do it,' Gumboot observed, 'so they lumber us with it. Some fucking deal!'

'*What's* that, Trooper?' The RSM had appeared from nowhere. He was standing there, large as life, in front of Gumboot and glaring at him. 'Did I hear a complaint?'

'Complaint, boss? No! No complaints. I think you must have misheard me.'

'If that word's in the English language,' Andrew said, 'I'll give up writing for good.'

'You couldn't write your name on a cheque, so get back to work,' the RSM said, marching away again.

'Yes, boss!' Andrew bawled.

And work he did. As did most of the others. Not through the whole night, but certainly until well after midnight, by when the last of the Skyvans had been and gone, letting silence descend at last with the settling dust.

Reprieved at last, the more fortunate men left the airstrip, leaving the unlucky few to stand guard on the loaded-up Bedfords. The former made their way back to the waste ground, where they shook everything out, then, still wearing their OGs, wriggled gratefully into their sleeping bags.

Ricketts closed his eyes, but could not sleep. There were too many whining mosquitoes, too many itchy places on his skin. Also, every time he drifted off, the image of his wife floated before him, jerking him awake. He tried to shut her out, to make his mind a blank, but the silence, which in fact was filled with rustling and shifting sounds, only drew him back to tormenting visions of her body and face.

Then Ricketts heard a ghostly moaning. At first he thought he was imagining it. Startled, then a little frightened, he opened his eyes. The moaning was growing louder; it gradually turned into a groaning. When Ricketts turned his head to the side, the sound had become almost anguished. It was coming from Andrew.

'What the fuck's the matter with you?' Ricketts heard Gumboot ask.

'Oh, man,' Andrew groaned, 'this is the worst time of all. I've got a hard-on that's as big as the Jebel and I can't stop thinking of tits and ass. It's a monster and it just won't go down and I'm trapped in this sleeping bag. Oh, man, this is awful.'

'Jesus Christ!' Gumboot said.

When Andrew moaned yet again, Ricketts smiled and at last dropped off to sleep.

9

At first light the following morning, the 250 men, including SAS, SAF and *firqats*, were driven out of the staging post in Bedfords, following a Saladin armoured car which had taken the lead position to give them some protection from mines. For added insurance against mines, the lengthy convoy drove cross-country, though parallel to the road.

The journey was hell, taking them across the Negd plain, a sun-scorched moonscape interlaced with dried-up stream beds, each of which caused the trucks to lurch wildly, as if about to topple over. In the rear of their Bedford, Ricketts and the other probationers, all in Sergeant Lampton's charge, were repeatedly thrown into each other, their weapons and water bottles colliding noisily. The Bedfords were open-topped, which at least meant they had air, but as the sun rose in the sky, casting a silvery light on the desert, they began to feel the heat and knew, with a feeling of unease, that it was going to get much worse. Surprisingly, even in the wind created by the truck's movement, the flies and mosquitoes were still present in abundance, buzzing and diving, growing more frantic the more the men sweated and attracted them.

'As long as I live I'm going to remember these little bastards,' Ricketts said, swiping another mosquito from his face. 'I've never seen so many of them in my life. They bloody torment me.'

'And me!' Andrew said.

'I thought you'd be used to them,' Gumboot said, ducking and weaving. 'What with where you come from and all.'

'Brixton,' Andrew said.

'I thought you said Barbados.'

'My *mother* comes from Barbados,' Andrew explained, slapping his own cheek, 'but I was born in Brixton.'

'You're going down in my estimation every minute. You're not even exotic!'

'Sorry, Gumboot.'

'I come from Smethwick,' Tom Purvis said helpfully, 'but the family then moved to Wolverhampton. I hope you think *that's* exotic.'

'Not as exotic as Pensett,' Bill Raglan said, 'which has a grammar school, a glassworks, a Miners' Welfare Club, and, of course, Wolverhampton Wanderers. How does that grab you?'

'I pity you,' Gumboot told him. 'But now at last I know why you're both halfwits – no stimulation.'

'There's lots of that in Devon, then? Lots of moo-moos and dung. Incest in the barns every Friday, followed by home-brewed cider. I feel deprived just thinking of it.'

'Christ,' Gumboot said, ignoring the dumb twat and slapping frantically at the mosquitoes and flies swarming around his face, 'these things are driving me crazy.'

'Your natural state,' Andrew said.

As usual, they relied on banter of this kind to keep the blues at bay, but as the morning wore on and the heat increased dramatically, making them sweat even more, thus attracting more flies and mosquitoes, they felt less inclined to crack jokes. Also, as the journey progressed, the gravel plain became rougher, filling up with patches of sand, and the bucking of the trucks became much worse.

By noon, the convoy was still on the move, with the Arabian sun blazing relentlessly on the desert and turning it into a featureless white haze. Heat waves rose from the desert floor, making the land beyond shimmer, and the trucks front and rear, when visible through the swirling sand, appeared to contract and expand, as if made from black jelly.

The men seemed just as unreal – or at least, they felt so – assailed by flies and mosquitoes, sometimes by stinging hornets, while being forced repeatedly to wipe grimy sweat from their faces or sand from their parched lips, bloodshot eyes, sweat-soaked clothing and hot-barrelled weapons. With the sand came the dust – floating everywhere, rising up through the floorboards, and blown in from the billowing clouds being churned up by the wheels of the Bedfords.

Even worse was the heat, now a veritable furnace, making even the slipstream of the trucks suffocatingly warm.

'I can hardly breathe,' Gumboot rasped. 'This air's thick with dust and sand. It's so warm, it makes me almost choke. I feel bloody nauseous.'

'So do I,' Tom said.

'My stomach's churning,' Bill added.

'They've got to stop and let us out for a bit,' Andrew insisted, looking out across the vast, sun-scorched plain and its drifting dust clouds. 'They've got to give us a break from this.'

'They won't,' Lampton said. 'We don't have the time. We've got to reach the RV by last light, so they won't have a break.'

'Oh, fuck!' Bill groaned, then closed his mouth and choked, his cheeks suddenly bulging, and clawed his way past Gumboot and

134

Tom to hang over the truck's tailboard and throw up.

'That was decent of him,' Lampton said as Bill continued vomiting, his body heaving convulsively. 'If he'd done it where he was sitting, it would have gone all over you lot. Now, at least, he's put it all behind us.'

Gumboot laughed uneasily at that, but a few minutes later, when Bill was back in his seat, gasping for breath and cleaning his messy lips with a handkerchief, Gumboot – either smelling Raglan or imagining he could smell him – was likewise suddenly obliged to claw his way to the rear and throw up over the tailboard. He was soon followed by Tom, then, as Ricketts noticed, by some of the men in the other Bedfords, front and rear, now distorted beyond the shimmering heat waves and obscured by the boiling sand.

'If anyone comes after us,' Lampton said, 'they won't have a problem. They've only to follow the trail of . . .'

'Do you mind?' Andrew interrupted.

'What's that?' Lampton asked.

'No offence, boss, but the mere mention of that word will just set them all off again.'

'Got you, Trooper,' Lampton said with a broad grin, clearly as fit as a fiddle and enjoying himself.

Though men continued being ill along the

whole length of the column, the drivers did, as Lampton had warned, keep going without a break. They reached the wadi by late afternoon, when the fierce white sun had cooled to a more mellow golden light that brought detail back to the landscape.

Glancing along the wadi, with its sheer granite slopes casting stark black shadows on the sun-bleached gravel of the valley floor – a barren, silent, almost eerie terrain – Ricketts was reminded of the boulders and craters of the moon, which he had seen on TV coverage of the Apollo 15 landing in July, three months earlier. This in turn reminded him that he was a long way from home and in a new, totally alien environment. It made him feel slightly disorientated and remote from himself.

Entering the wadi, heading straight for the towering Jebel, the lengthy column of trucks soon left the sand-filled Negd behind and drove over a smoother surface of tightly packed gravel and small stones. Mercifully, the shadows cast over the convoy by the high rock faces on either side brought the men further protection from the sun and wind. Eventually the sun went down, cooling the men even more.

'Thank God for the evening,' Ricketts said. 'A little relief at last.'

'It'll soon be so fucking cold you'll have frost

on your nuts,' Gumboot replied. 'If it isn't one thing, it's another. This place is a pisser.'

Now out of the wind and dust, the men were removing the magazines from their SLRs and other weapons to clean them again, working the cocking handles to ensure that they were back in good order. Some were hurrying to finish this task when the convoy ground to a halt because the wadi had narrowed so much that they would have to go the rest of the way by foot.

Ricketts placed a 7.62mm round back in the magazine of his SLR, fixed the magazine to the weapon and cocked the action. He had time to quickly squeeze oil onto the side of the breech before following the other troopers out of the Bedford.

Standing on the gravel floor of the wadi as the other SAS, SAF and *firqats* also jumped down, rapidly filling up the formerly empty, silent area, he was surprised to see Sergeant 'Dead-eye Dick' Parker with a nearby group, still wearing his jellaba and *shemagh*, which, with his bandoliers and two knives, made him look as fearsome as the tribesmen. In fact, even as Ricketts saw him, he moved away from the SAS group and went to join the Arabs, talking to them in a low murmur and receiving solemn nods from them by way of reply.

'Fucking Lawrence of Arabia,' Gumboot said.

'And probably just as mad,' Andrew added.

'A damned good soldier,' Lampton informed them. 'At least the *firqats* respect him.'

'They respect men as mad as they are.' Gumboot was checking his M16. 'They know he'd slit your throat as quick as look at you. That's what they respect.'

'OK, you men!' RSM Worthington bawled, standing mere feet away, his barrel chest heaving. 'Don't stand there like limp dicks at a wedding. Clean out those Bedfords!'

The equipment was unloaded and divided among the men. As number two of the GPMG sustained-fire team, Ricketts would be carrying a steel tripod weighing over 30lb, plus a thousand rounds of 7.62mm ammunition belts — half wrapped around his body, the other half in his bergen — and four 20-round SLR magazines on his belt. He also had his Browning handgun, belt kit with smoke and fragmentation grenades, rations, first-aid kit, and three full water bottles. Also in his team were Jock as gun controller, Gumboot as observer and Andrew as number one, or trigger man. Between them, apart from personal gear, they had to hump the tripod, two spare barrels weighing 6lb each, spare return spring, dial sight, marker pegs, two aiming posts, aiming lamp, recoil buffer, tripod sighting bracket, spare-parts wallet, and the gun itself, weighing 24lb. Burdened with all this, they would have to climb out of the wadi, up onto the flat, open area of the Mahazair Pools, which was their night basha spot.

'This is gonna fucking kill us,' Jock McGregor said.

Gumboot studied the Arab fighters conversing solemnly with Dead-eye Parker. 'Those bastards aren't carrying much,' he said. 'Only personal weapons.'

'They don't need as much as us,' Lampton explained. 'They'll be out front, facing the *adoo*, while we give them covering fire. Let that console you.'

'Donkey soldiers,' Andrew said. 'Isn't that what they call us? Because we hump all this heavy gear. *Donkey soldiers*! The bastards must be having a good laugh at us.'

'If I hear any of them calling me that, I'll give them what for.'

'Since you don't speak their language, Gumboot, you won't hear a damned thing,' Andrew corrected him.

'Prepare to saddle up!' the RSM bellowed. 'We haven't got all night!'

In preparation for the climb, Ricketts unlocked the front leg-clamp levers of the GPMG tripod, swung them forward into the high-mount position and relocked them. Then, with Andrew's help, he humped the tripod up onto his shoulders with the front legs resting on his chest and the rear one trailing backwards over his bergen. His total burden now weighed a crippling 130lb, and he was carrying his SLR with his free hand.

All along the wadi, in the dimming afternoon light, the other men were doing the same, making a hell of a racket. There were 250 of them in all, spread out over approximately a quarter of a mile, between and around the parked Bedfords.

'OK, men,' Worthington bellowed, his voice reverberating eerily around the wadi, as if amplified. 'Saddle up!'

The men moved out, falling instinctively into a lengthy, irregular file formation, spreading more and more apart, until the line was a good half mile long, snaking back from the slopes of the wadi to the trucks below.

Within minutes, the metal of the tripod cradle was digging viciously into the back of Ricketts's neck, letting him know that it was going to hurt. He turned his head left and right, but this only rubbed the skin of his neck against the steel leg, making it hurt even more. In less than an hour the pain was worse, shooting down through his shoulder blades, and the sweat was starting from his forehead and dripping into his eyes.

He glanced at his nearest friends and saw

that they were suffering the same — if not with a tripod, certainly with other gear — and sweating every bit as much as he was. No one spoke. They were trying to save their breath. To make the hike more tortuous, they were assailed, as usual, by flies, mosquitoes and the occasional hornet, but this time they could not slap them away as they were either carrying weapons or holding onto heavy equipment, just as Ricketts had to do with his tripod. Now it was hurting more than ever, sending darting pains through his shoulders, and those pains, combined with his increasing exhaustion, made him start wondering if he could actually stand the strain.

Ricketts's fears were in no way eased when, one after the other, a number of troopers vomited from the strain and were pulled out of the column and ordered by the RSM to 'rest up, then catch up'. This brought no respite to the others, since the column continued moving. However, it stopped shortly after, the men banging into one another, as voices called down the line for the medics. When those voices faded away, a series of hand signals came down the line, indicating that the men were to rest up until further notice. Gratefully, the men around Ricketts all sank to the ground.

'What's up?' Ricketts asked.

'I don't know,' Lampton replied, 'but I'm going to find out.'

As the sergeant hurried away towards the front end of the column, Gumboot wriggled out of his bergen and lay on his back.

'Ah, God,' he said breathlessly, 'that's wonderful. That's just bloody beautiful.'

Andrew wiped sweat from his gleaming black forehead as he lay back with his head on his bergen. 'I don't give a shit what's happened, so long as it buys a rest.'

'Which it has,' Ricketts said.

'I've thrown up twice already,' Tom told them, 'and I still don't feel too good.'

'Who does?' Bill asked rhetorically. 'Not me, mate.'

They fell silent after that, trying to get their breath back, not wanting Lampton to return and make them get up again. Unfortunately, he did so five minutes later.

'Heart attack,' he said. 'A radio corporal. He collapsed with his radio, got stuck between some rocks, and had a heart attack trying to free himself. He's conscious again, but he's going to have to be carried on a stretcher to the RV, from where he can be casevacked back to base.'

'Lucky bastard,' Tom said.

'The poor bastards who have to carry him

aren't so lucky,' Lampton replied. 'OK, men, on your feet.'

'What?' Andrew's head jerked around. 'You mean we're moving already?' Lampton nodded towards the front of the line. When they all turned in that direction, they saw a series of hand signals coming towards them, indicating that the march was recommencing. 'Shit!' Andrew exclaimed.

Luckily, they were near the end of their journey. They had been marching for two hours and the sun was going down. After another three-quarters of an hour the slopes became less steep, indicating that they were nearly out of the wadi. Eventually, as the sun sank, a breeze, blowing down from the level ground, cooled the sweat on their foreheads.

Ricketts was beginning to believe that he was on his last legs – stabbing pains in his shoulder blades, his neck aching, his lungs on fire – when, just before darkness fell, they emerged from the wadi and headed across an open area, where pale moonlight was reflected off the water in the Mahazair Pools, in the shadow of the mighty Jebel Dhofar.

They could rest up at last.

10

The rest only lasted a few minutes. At last light, with the eerie wailing of the mullah rending the silence, the *firqats*, their faces half hidden by *shemaghs*, knelt in circles and bowed their heads to pray while holding their rifles between their knees.

'I don't think we can depend on these geezers,' Gumboot whispered out of the corner of his mouth to Ricketts and Andrew. 'They're not allowed to fight during the holy month of Ramadan – and that's due to begin later this month.'

'Right,' Andrew said, nodding. 'But these guys have been let off on the grounds that they're Islamic warriors fighting a Holy War.'

'That's convenient,' Ricketts said.

'And the fact that they're praying right now,' Sergeant Lampton informed them, 'is a sign that Operation Jaguar's about to begin.'

'What, already?' Bill asked, glancing automatically up at the mighty Jebel, then across at the *firqats* kneeling in prayer, their rounded shoulders bathed in the moonlight when they bowed their covered heads.

'Yes,' Lampton said. 'Already. We have to make the climb tonight, under cover of darkness.'

'There's no way we can do that,' Tom said. 'Not after a day like the one we've put in. It's asking too much.'

'Do you want to keep that badge or don't you?' Lampton asked him.

'You know the answer to that, boss.'

'Then it's not asking too much. Zero hour is thirty minutes from now and you'd best be prepared.'

Realizing that they were actually going to have to get up and go, the men drank more mugs of tea, cleaned and oiled their weapons, filled magazines and water bottles, and stared curiously at the still kneeling, praying tribesmen, now bathed in the moonlight. Beyond them, near one of the pools, was the collection of tents and lean-tos of the SAS base camp that had been established here a few weeks before. Some of the troopers were outside their tents, brewing up in the open.

'I don't envy them their job,' Andrew said,

glancing at the men in the base camp. 'Stuck up here for weeks on end with sweet fuck all to do.'

'It's good training for OP work,' Lampton told him, 'and you'll get plenty of that in the future. That's why you had all that psychological flak during Sickener Two – to prepare you for days, sometimes weeks on end, in an observation post with only yourselves for company and not much to do, other than keep tabs on enemy movements. It's the worst, the most difficult, job of all.'

'It couldn't be worse than climbing the Jebel,' Jock insisted.

'Don't even think about that,' Lampton warned him. 'It won't help you a bit. You'll just give up before you start.'

Glancing up at the vast, imposing plateau, now almost jet-black and ringed by stars in the gathering darkness, Ricketts was reminded of his last night on the Pen-y-fan, during Sickener Two, and had a good idea of the tortures awaiting him.

The thought was disturbing, but also undeniably exciting, a contradiction of emotions that he had learned to live with ever since he had worked on the North Sea oil rigs. He was not a hard man, nor did he think himself cruel, but he definitely had a low boredom threshold and the need for adventure.

146

Thank God Maggie understood that. His wife was a treasure. Like Ricketts in that she was sentimental and romantic, she missed him not being at home a lot, but was satisfied that he was not fooling around when out of her sight. She knew him enough to know that he was not that kind of man, but merely needed the kind of excitement that normal life did not offer. The line between that need and the love of violence was thin, but, as Maggie well understood, her husband was on the right side of it. Though understanding the moral ambiguity of what he was doing, Ricketts could not still his urge for adventure, no matter how dangerous. So, he accepted it, while remaining wary of it, careful not to let it run amok.

Nevertheless, only when he experienced that odd combination of fear and excitement – as he was doing right now, in the shadow of the mighty Jebel – did Ricketts feel truly, electrically alive. This was a truth he could not deny.

'Any minute now,' Lampton said, checking his wristwatch. 'In fact, any *second* now.'

He was right. It was now completely dark, with no sign of the moon, and the sudden sound of equipment being moved in the *firqats'* area indicated that the operation was under way.

Clambering to his feet with the others, Ricketts checked his kit and weapons, then again let

Andrew help him hump the heavy GPMG tripod
onto his shoulders. The rear leg bit immediately
into his neck, reminding him of what he was in
for, but also making him resolve to endure it,
no matter what the cost.

The *firqat* guides led off in the darkness, heading south-east, and the rest of the assault force,
including the SAF, now all wearing *shemaghs*
instead of berets, followed in a single file that
gradually stretched out to form an immense
human chain, snaking up the lower slopes
of the Jebel. At first the slopes were gentle,
presenting no real challenge, but soon they
rose more steeply, sometimes almost vertically,
turning the hike into a mountain climb that
tortured body and mind. The steeper gradients
were often smooth, making the men slip and
slide, and often, where the gradients were less
steep, loose gravel led to the same problems. A
lot of cursing passed down the line. Men fell and
rolled downhill. The climb was made no easier
by the moonless darkness, which hid dangerous
outcrops and crevices. The column nevertheless
continued to snake upwards, making slow, painful progress.

'Take five,' were the words passed down the
line an hour later, by which time most of the
men were sweating, out of breath and aching
all over.

Removing the tripod, Ricketts slumped to the ground with the others and, like them, gratefully gulped water from one of his three, rapidly emptying bottles.

'God,' he said, 'this is murderous.'

'It's what we joined for,' Andrew reminded him.

'I can't remember why I wanted the badge,' Gumboot said. 'I must have been mad.'

Still gasping for breath and soaked in his own sweat, Ricketts glanced along the line and saw Sergeant Parker squatting on the ground near the *firqats*, dressed just like them, as impassive as them, and not displaying one drop of sweat.

'Right,' Andrew whispered. 'Don't say it. I know just what you're thinking. That bastard, Dead-eye Dick, is sitting there as cool as a cucumber, not fazed at all.'

'He's not normal, that bastard,' Gumboot said. 'I'd lay odds he's a fucking psychopath. He gets his kicks out of suffering.'

'How good do you think he really is?' Ricketts asked no one in particular.

'He's exceptional,' Lampton told him. 'He's as good a marksman as any *adoo* – and that's saying a lot.'

'Thanks, Sarge,' Andrew said, 'for those encouraging words. It's nice to know that we're going up against an enemy that shoots better than we do.'

'No point in telling lies.'

'Little white lies have their moments.'

'In this kind of war,' Lampton insisted, 'it's best to know what you're up against. And the *adoo*, believe me, are good. They have the eyes of eagles.'

'Fucking wonderful,' Gumboot said. 'That's all I need to know. After killing ourselves climbing this bloody mountain, we'll get picked off like flies. Let's all kneel in prayer.'

Five minutes later, they were on the move again, killing themselves as they slogged up the ever-steeper mountainside, slipping and sliding in loose gravel or on smooth stone, catching their feet in fissures, banging their heads or elbows against outcrops hidden in darkness.

For the next five hours, they halted every hour and wetted their parched throats with more water. They soon began to run short.

'According to the *firqats*,' Lampton said, 'there was a well four hours march from the Mahazair Pools. We've now been on the march for five hours and there's still no sign of it.'

'Apart from knowing how to slit enemy throats,' Bill said, 'those A-rabs don't know a damned thing.'

'They better,' Lampton said, 'because they're the ones guiding us up this mountain.'

'I'll believe it when we see it,' Tom said, 'and I don't think we'll see it.'

'Let's hope that at least they find the well,' Andrew said, 'before our water runs out.'

'I'm low,' Ricketts said.

'So am I,' Gumboot told him.

'Stop talking about it,' Lampton advised them, 'and you won't feel so thirsty. Also, you won't feel so breathless. You've still got a long climb ahead of you, so try conserving your breath.'

An hour later, after six hours of climbing, they halted again – unfortunately not for the well, but because another of the men, laden with three radios and marching right in front of Ricketts, suddenly choked, vomited and collapsed.

Andrew, who had had special medical training, dropped immediately to his knees beside the unconscious man, loosened his webbing, removed the radios and other heavy kit, then hammered on his chest in an attempt to revive him. When this failed, he applied mouth-to-mouth resuscitation, but this was also to no avail. Without thinking about his own diminishing supply, Andrew opened the only one of his three bottles still containing water and poured some down the unconscious trooper's throat. The man coughed and spluttered back

151

to dazed consciousness just as Major Greenaway and RSM Worthington appeared on the scene, having walked back from the front of the column.

'Christ!' Greenaway exclaimed in frustration. 'Not another heart attack!'

'Don't know, boss,' Andrew said, 'but whatever it is, it's not fatal. He's not in the best condition, but he's conscious and I think he'll be OK.'

'Can he walk?'

'I wouldn't ask him to try just yet.'

Greenaway turned to Worthington. 'If we call in a casevac chopper, we could compromise the whole operation. We'll have to send him back to the base camp. From there, he can be casevacked back to RAF Salalah.'

'That means a stretcher, boss, and two men carrying it. No easy job on this mountain.'

'We're not here for easy jobs, Bob, so get this man on a stretcher.'

'Yes, boss, will do.' As Greenaway marched back to the head of the column, a lot higher up the mountain, the RSM looked around him, then jabbed his forefinger at two troopers. 'You and you,' he said.

'Aw, shit, no!' one of the men protested.

'Right, boss,' the other said. 'We've been through hell to get this far and now you're sending us back. It isn't fair, boss.'

'It isn't a question of fairness,' Worthington replied. 'It's a matter of necessity. We can't afford to lose any medics before the battle commences, so he has to be taken down by two troopers and I've chosen you.'

'Why us?'

'You happen to be nearest. Now shut up and wait until I send down a stretcher. Then take this man back to base.'

A few minutes after the RSM had hiked back up the mountain, towards the front of the column, two medics came down with a rolled-up stretcher. After unrolling it, they hoisted the groaning trooper onto it, then turned to the men chosen by the RSM to carry him back to base.

'OK,' a medic said, 'he's all yours.'

'He *should* be all yours,' one of the troopers replied.

The medic shrugged and grinned. 'It's all in the lap of the gods, meaning the lap of the RSM. Have a good trip, lads.'

Before the troopers could reply, the medics hurried back uphill. The troopers, looking disgusted, hoisted the stretcher up between them. 'Fucking diabolical,' one of them said, as they started downhill with the groaning man.

'OK,' Lampton said, 'let's move out again.'

Knowing that first light would be at 0530

hours, Greenaway marched his men mercilessly, following the hardy *firqats* uphill through the darkness, still with no sign of the promised well and its life-giving water. Even at this time of the morning, in that total, moonless darkness, the heat was considerable, clammy, suffocating and rendered worse by the dust kicked up by hundreds of marching feet. More men choked and were sick.

Ricketts began to suffer from heat exhaustion and dehydration: dry mouth and throat, swollen tongue, cracked lips. He also began to hear lurking *adoo* with every sound and to see them in the dark outlines of rocks and outcrops. Aware that the *adoo* were superb marksmen, able to pick off enemy troops at distances so great they had been called the 'phantom enemy', his imaginings along these lines became increasingly vivid.

As they pressed on, the *firqats* up front decided to lighten their heavy loads by discarding valuable items of kit, such as ration cans, portable hexamine cookers and blocks of hexamine fuel. These littered the upward trail and made the going even more difficult for the SAS troops behind them. When reprimanded by RSM Worthington, the Arabs started screaming angrily, threw their weapons and kit to the ground, and threatened to return to the base camp. Appeased by their diplomatic friend,

Dead-eye Dick Parker, they picked up what they had just thrown down and continued the march.

'Selfish fucking bastards!' Gumboot managed to groan between anguished breaths.

Nevertheless, the climb continued, with more men collapsing and either being revived and made to keep going or, if they were in serious condition, sent back to the base camp.

About half an hour before first light, the men ahead began disappearing one by one over the skyline, filling Ricketts with the hope that this must be the top of the plateau.

In fact, it was a false crest, only leading down into another wadi. The men gathered together at the bottom of that wadi just as dawn's light appeared in the east. At the head of his hundred men, but behind the SAF and *firqats*, Major Greenaway consulted with RSM Worthington, both of them studying their maps by torchlight, neither looking pleased.

'We should have been on Lympne by now,' Greenaway said loudly, in exasperation. 'Those *firqat* guides have led us in the wrong direction. We should be on high ground.' He glanced angrily at the masked guides. 'Those stupid bloody . . .' Not wanting to cause trouble with the notoriously proud and temperamental Arab fighters, he let his voice trail off, scratched his chin in deep thought, then turned to the RSM. 'Go and talk to the scouts,' he said. 'Find out just where we are.'

The RSM went off, embroiled himself in a heated discussion with the *firqat* guides, then had a talk with the fearsome-looking Sergeant Parker. The latter nodded, then hurried away, clambering up the steep face of the wadi with the agility of a mountain goat, eventually disappearing in the darkness. When he had gone, the RSM, looking frustrated, returned to Greenaway.

'Those bloody *firqats* aren't sure where the track leading to Lympne is, so I've sent Sergeant Parker on ahead to do a recce. He's the best tracker we've got and if anyone can find the trail, he can.'

'Right,' Greenaway replied. 'We might as well make the most of the opportunity. Tell the men to take five.'

In a state of exhaustion made worse by lack of sleep, the men squatted on the ground as best they could while still wearing their bergens. As even glowing cigarettes could betray their position to the enemy, they were not allowed to smoke, but they compensated for this lack with chocolate and chewing gum, and by releasing their frustration over the *firqats*.

'Fucking typical!' Gumboot exploded. 'We've

been trained for this kind of work, but they leave it to the A-rabs and before you can say boo we're lost. I could piss on their heads!'

'I wouldn't try it,' Andrew said. 'They might chop your dick off. Not that you'd even realize it was missing, given what you've not done with it – but still, it might hurt.'

'It's no joke,' said Bill. 'I side with Gumboot here. I've heard a lot about these *firqats* and none of it was good, so I don't see why we're supposed to depend on them.'

'It's because *they* know the mountains,' Tom said sarcastically. 'That's why we're all sitting here on our arses, with not a clue where we are – the dependable *firqats*.'

'So one of our own men goes on ahead to find out where the trail is,' Gumboot said, spitting to emphasise his contempt.

'Fucking choice, ain't it? It all gets back to us. And I suppose if Dead-eye *does* find the track, those *firqat* bastards will go on strike.'

'They're not that bad,' Lampton said.

'I've heard they go on strike, boss.'

'There are times when they down arms and turn to prayer instead, but given that we're in a Muslim country, you have to accept that. It's not like going on strike.'

'Same difference to me.'

'You lack a world view, Gumboot.'

'I lack patience with any fucking scout who gets me lost in the mountains. What a malarkey!'

A lot of the men's aggravation was due to exhaustion, but that didn't make it any less real. Luckily, they were only there fifteen minutes before Parker returned to say he had found what he thought was the track leading up to Lympne.

An hour later, ninety minutes after they should have been there, and just after the sun had risen, they arrived, with churning stomachs and aching muscles, on the plateau of the mighty Jebel Dhofar.

11

As expected, the scrub ground being used as a makeshift *adoo* airstrip was deserted. This was confirmation that the other SAS troop's diversionary attack to the south had been successful in drawing the *adoo* away – hopefully long enough for the assault force to get entrenched above and around the airstrip, where they would wait for the enemy to return.

Nevertheless, receiving instructions from a combination of radio messages and hand signals, the 250 men sank to the ground in a line that snaked in an enormous arc around the airstrip. Major Greenaway then moved the assault group, team by team, across the open ground, meeting no resistance whatsoever.

Lying belly-down on the ground, watching the mass of men advance towards the airstrip in small groups, jumping up and darting forward under cover of the others, then dropping down and jumping up again, Ricketts had the chance to study the terrain in the dawn light. Around the makeshift airstrip there were rocky, parched hills, but on the flatlands, on high elevations, he could see other improvised runways and water gleaming in the area's few watering-holes. It was the latter, he knew, that made this area so valuable to the *adoo*, and they would certainly fight fiercely to defend it. The airfields were little more than strips of level ground, levelled more carefully by hand, and surrounded by defensive trenches and the occasional hut of wood or corrugated iron. There were no control towers or even watch-towers. As for this particular airfield, known as Lympne, the *adoo*, in their zeal to defeat the SAS's diversionary attack to the south, had failed to leave even one man on guard. It was completely deserted.

'They may be crack marksmen,' Andrew said, 'but they can't be that bright.'

'They don't have to be too bright,' Gumboot said. 'They're fucking ferocious. That's what makes them hard to beat.'

'Still, it's kind of them,' Ricketts said, 'to leave us this whole airstrip for our own use. Presumably that's where the rest of the assault force is going to land.'

'That's right,' Bill said. 'That's the LZ – presuming the rest of the assault force manages to get here before the *adoo* return.'

Lampton, who had been in consultation with Greenaway, came crawling up to them with his M16 cradled in his arms. 'Right,' he said. 'I want the machine-gun team to take up a position on the eastern flank of the airstrip, halfway up that hill overlooking it. You can build yourselves a sangar up there and turn it into a nice home from home. The rest of you will stay with me, taking up a position lower down the same slope. The SAF and *firqats* will be leading the advance against the *adoo* and we'll give covering fire. OK, lads, get going.'

With practically no rest, the very thought of climbing to his feet so soon filled Ricketts with weariness. But he did so, shouldering the tripod again with Andrew's help, then leading him, Gumboot and Jock towards the hills rising east of the airstrip. The hike was longer than anticipated, taking almost an hour, and when they finally arrived at their position they were sweaty and breathless.

From here they had a panoramic view of the nearby hills and the valleys far below. The SAF and *firqats* had completely surrounded the airstrip. SAS troops were marking the runway with coloured smoke grenades for the reinforcements being flown in. It was now 0815 and the grey light of morning was growing brighter, creating a jigsaw of shadow and light over the parched hills and plains.

'Quite a view,' Andrew said, scribbling in his notebook. 'It was worth that hellish climb just to see this. My soul soars like an eagle.'

'Stash that notebook,' Ricketts said, 'and let's build a sangar. Then we can fix the machine-gun and brew up and have us some breakfast.'

'Sounds good to me,' Gumboot said.

Downing their bergens and kit, Ricketts, Andrew and Gumboot started to build the sangar by wrenching boulders out of the ground with their bare hands and stacking them in a rough circle. Meanwhile, Jock kept watch and also listened for incoming calls on the PRC 319.

The sangar took the shape of a semicircular drystone wall three feet high and eight feet in diameter. When it was completed, the men laid their bergens, kit and personal weapons around the inner wall, then mounted the machine-gun, placing the tripod on its triangular legs and relocking the clamp levers. After levelling the cradle for a good firing angle, Ricketts withdrew the front mounting pin. Jock had already serviced the gun for mounting, with the gas-regulator correctly set and the recoil buffer fitted. He now inserted the rear mounting pin into the body of the GPMG, lifted the gun into position on the cradle slot projection, pushed it fully forward, then locked it with the front mounting pin. With the gun prepared, Andrew, the trigger man, was able to open the top cover, load a belt of 200 rounds, cock the action and apply the safety catch.

'So,' he said, sitting back against the wall of the sangar, 'she's all set to go.'

Glancing over the wall, down the hillside, Ricketts saw that many other SAS teams had constructed similar sangars on the slopes overlooking three sides of the airstrip and were covering it with L7A2 GPMGs, M-72 LAWs and L16 ML 81mm mortars. Below him, some 2000 yards down the hill, Sergeant Lampton was sharing a sangar with troopers Purvis and Raglan, as well as a two-man mortar team. Not far to the right, all on his own, the dangerously eccentric Dead-eye Dick Parker was smoking a cigarette, studying the landscape and resting his free hand on the L42A1 7.62mm Lee Enfield sniper rifle lying on the wall of his small, one-man sangar. At the very bottom of the hill, on the level ground around the airstrip, SAF, *firqat* and Baluchi troops had taken over the unprotected *adoo* defensive trenches and appeared to be eating and drinking contentedly.

'Let's have a brew-up,' Ricketts said.

'No water left,' Gumboot replied, spitting over the wall of the sangar. 'We're all dry as a bone.'

'Shit,' said Jock in disgust.

'The back-up force is arriving,' Andrew told them. 'Let's hope they've brought water.'

Ricketts spotted the first of the Skyvans appearing in the sky to the south. Soon the air was filled with them as lift after lift came in, followed by Huey and Sikorski helicopters. One after the other, they landed on the airstrip improvised by the absent *adoo*, their propellers and rotors whipping up enormous, billowing clouds of dust that obscured the men pouring out of the aircraft and across the runway, carrying artillery pieces, mortars, ammunition, rations and, most important of all, water.

By the time the last of the aircraft had landed, the assault force had reached a total strength of 800 men, including 100 SAS, 250 SAF, 300 *firqat* members and 150 Baluchi tribesmen.

Just as they had arrived, so the aircraft took off one by one, creating more clouds of dust. While Ricketts and the others were watching this spectacle, an SAS trooper with an M16 across his back, obviously one of the new arrivals, laboriously climbed the hill, bringing with him two jerrycans of water. Reaching the sangar, he placed the jerrycans on the ground and puffed, 'What a hike! Who's got a cigarette?'

'It's the least we can offer you,' Gumboot said, giving the man a cigarette from his own packet. 'Sit down. We're just about to brew up.'

'Thanks,' the new man said, taking the cigarette and accepting a light from Gumboot. 'I'm bloody exhausted already.' He sat on the ground beside Gumboot. 'And I haven't even climbed the Jebel,' he said, blowing a cloud of smoke. 'What was it like?'

'It could have been worse,' Gumboot said modestly. 'But it was pretty exhausting.'

'I'll bet,' the new man said. 'I'm Dave Greaves, by the way.'

Gumboot introduced himself and the others as Jock set up his hexamine stove and boiled water in his mess tin. The others took out their tin mugs and put tea bags in them, waiting for the water to boil.

'Any news from down below?' Ricketts asked.

'Not much,' Greaves replied, inhaling and blowing another cloud of smoke. 'Apparently, the diversionary attack to the south was a success, drawing the *adoo* away from here and resulting in no SAS casualties. The attack's over now, though, and the *adoo* are believed to be on their way back. Expect fireworks very soon.'

When the water had boiled, Jock poured it into the five tin mugs set out on the ground. The men then added sugar and powdered milk from packets, and sat back to enjoy their brew-up.

'So what's happening about food?' Gumboot asked, glancing down over the wall to where the SAF, *firqat* and Baluchi troops, spread out around the airfield, were having breakfast. The last of the aircraft and helicopters had taken off, leaving the dust to settle back down over the airstrip and the trenches formerly used by the *adoo*.

'I was told to tell you to use the high-calorie rations in your escape belts. They'll be replaced later in the day with fresh rations brought in on the Skyvans. The field kitchens won't be set up until later in the day, so you won't get a proper meal till tonight.'

'And even that may not happen,' Ricketts said, 'if the *adoo* attack.'

'Fucking wonderful!' Gumboot exclaimed. 'Meanwhile, those A-rabs down there are having a banquet.'

'They brought their own food,' Andrew pointed out, 'and I don't think you'd eat it.'

'Damned right, I wouldn't,' Gumboot replied. 'It's good old British tucker for me. I don't want to poison myself.'

'Then have your dry breakfast and shut up. Thank God for small mercies.'

'Hallelujah!' Jock said.

After finishing his tea, Trooper Greaves waved goodbye and headed back down the hill to his own position. He had not reached Lampton's sangar when the whole hill erupted.

12

The first explosions lacerated the ground near Greaves, showering him in soil and then picking him up and hurling him sideways. He hit the ground like a rag doll, bouncing off it, limbs flapping, before becoming lost in swirling smoke and more raining soil as the ground erupted again.

'Christ!' Ricketts exclaimed, ducking down behind the sangar wall and automatically picking up his SLR. More explosions ripped the hillside, making a catastrophic din, as Ricketts stared at the others, all of whom were staring back, then tentatively raised his head above the wall to look out again. A stream of green tracer, surprisingly luminous in the morning light, snaked out of the boiling smoke, first appearing to almost float, then zipping overhead at fantastic speed to spend itself a good distance away. Another series of explosions erupted across the hillside, spewing earth and more smoke.

'The *adoo*!' Andrew yelled, huddling up beside Ricketts with his M16 propped up between his knees.

'Right,' Ricketts said. Holding his SLR, he hugged the wall as the western perimeter came alive with the stutter of incoming small-arms fire. Raising his head again, he saw that the tracer was coming from the rim of the western hillside. The *adoo* GPMGs, he reckoned, were located just beyond that rim, as were their mortars. Even as he deduced this, a series of explosions erupted in a line that ran from the airstrip to the base of the eastern hill, tearing through the defensive trenches in which the SAF troops were now sheltering. More soil spewed upwards and rained down through the clouds of black smoke.

'Mother of God,' Jock whispered. 'Those bastards aren't fooling!'

Lower down the hill, Greaves, miraculously still alive, was raising himself up on hands and knees, shaking his head to clear it. Soil dropped off his arched back as he vomited convulsively, then another explosion tore up the earth beside him and flipped him over again.

'Shit!' Gumboot hissed, then darted out of the sangar. He was starting down the hill when he was stopped by another burst of green tracer, which, whipping just above his head, made him throw himself to the ground.

'Gumboot!' Ricketts bawled.

'We've got to help him!' Gumboot shouted back while lying belly-down on the ground with tracers ripping through the air above him. 'That poor bastard is . . .'

His last words were drowned by the roar of another explosion that made the sangar shake and rained soil on it. Andrew was up and over the wall, even as the smoke blew in. He careered the few yards to Gumboot, and helped him back to his feet.

'Damn it, Gumboot, he's too far away! Get back in the sangar!'

They raced back to the sangar as more explosions erupted around them, causing soil to rain down and filling the air with dense smoke. They piled back into the sangar, crouching beside Ricketts and Jock as the shelling continued.

Using the PRC 319, Jock contacted base, located by the airstrip, and requested a medic to be sent up. The reply was affirmative. As Jock put the phone down, another series of mortar explosions tore up the hill below.

'Fucking hell!' Gumboot gasped.

'Keep your head down,' Andrew told him.

Gumboot reached for the GPMG, wanting to retaliate, but Ricketts slapped his hand off, saying, 'No! They're too far away. We can't do much from here. It's up to the others.'

'Who?' Andrew asked.

'The ones dug in on the western slope. They'll be the first to be attacked if the *adoo* advance.' Glancing over the wall, he saw the wavering green lines of tracer coming towards him, whipping above him, while more explosions erupted along the airstrip and on the lower slopes of the hill below. 'But they're not advancing at the moment,' he continued. 'In fact, there isn't a sign of them. The foot soldiers are obviously grouped beyond the rim of the western hill, but they're staying put while their mortars and machine-guns soften us up. Right now we can't do a thing. We just have to sit tight.'

'Fuck,' said Jock. Joining Ricketts, he looked over the wall as more explosions obscured Greaves in smoke and showered soil all around. When the smoke had cleared, Greaves was still there, flat on his back, almost certainly unconscious.

Two SAS medics were scrambling up the hill towards the trooper, one with a rolled-up stretcher on one shoulder, the older man shouldering a packed medical bag. Another series of explosions forced the pair to the ground, but when the turbulence died away they jumped up and completed their run. While one examined

Greaves, the other rolled out the stretcher. The latter fell onto his belly as more green tracer whipped through the air above him, and then he jumped up again and helped his friend roll Greaves onto the stretcher. They hurried back down the hill, carrying Greaves between them, as more explosions erupted all around them. They disappeared in the swirling smoke.

'Good men,' Ricketts whispered.

The attack continued for another twenty minutes, with the mortars hitting the western hill, the area between the trenches by the airstrip and the lower slopes of the hill itself, where SAF troops were also entrenched and returning the fire with their own GPMGs and 81mm mortars. Soon, the whole area was covered in a grey pall of smoke punctuated by criss-crossing lines of green tracer from the *adoo* and the purplish tracer of the SAF, SAS and other troops.

'Might as well finish our tea,' Andrew said. 'Not much else we can do.'

'True enough,' Ricketts replied.

They sipped hot tea as the green tracers continued to streak over the sangar and more explosions occurred lower down the slope. Occasionally, through the drifting smoke on the western perimeter, they saw SAF troops, including the *firqats* and backed by covering fire from the

SAS, making their way uphill, trying to get closer to the *adoo* hidden beyond the rim. However, long before they reached it the *adoo*'s attack slackened until only sporadic firing could be heard. Gradually even this died away and silence descended.

Glancing down the slope, Ricketts saw a couple of SAS troopers loping across the airstrip, from the western side, then up the hill to the sangar. It took them a long time to complete the journey and when finally they arrived, they were breathless.

'And I thought I was a fit man!' one of the troopers said, gasping. 'I'm Roy Baker and this' – he indicated the other soldier with a jerk of his thumb – 'is Taff Burgess, of A Squadron. Shit, what a hike!'

'Have a cup of tea,' said Ricketts.

'Appreciate it,' Baker replied, still gasping. He and Burgess slumped to the ground inside the sangar, both leaning back against the wall until tin mugs of steaming tea were in their hands. Breathing normally again, they drank gratefully, then lit up cigarettes.

'So what's happening over there?' Ricketts asked.

'Are you guys probationers?'

'Yes.'

'Your sergeant must have a lot of faith in

you, letting you run this machine-gun post unsupervised.'

'He's just down the slope a bit,' Ricketts explained, 'and we're in radio contact.'

'Still, he must trust you,' Baker said, sipping more tea. 'A very nice brew, this.'

'So what's happening?' Andrew asked.

'A force of between twenty and thirty *adoo* hit the positions over on the west with AK-47s and RPD light machine-guns as back-up. The SAF took no casualties, but had two hits, which makes us one up.'

'Why has the attack tapered off?'

'We think the *adoo* were just testing our strength. Some of the SAF got over the rim of the hill and found them already gone. The generally received wisdom is that they've retired to their stronghold at Jibjat, six kilometres west of here. That's where we're going tomorrow.'

'Why?' Ricketts asked.

'Because the Head Shed,' Baker replied, referring to their CO, Major Greenaway, 'thinks that makeshift airstrip down there, on Lympne, is fucking useless. Apparently it's already breaking up from this morning's resup landings. So tomorrow, at first light, we're going to march on Jibjat.'

'That's only 7500 yards away.'

'Right,' Baker said with a grin. 'A short hike to the enemy.'

'Who dares wins,' Ricketts said.

Before first light, after a night in the sangar during which they took one-hour turns on watch, or stag, they packed their bergens and prepared the GPMG and tripod for carriage. They destroyed their sangar, dismantling it brick by brick, then moved down the hill to join Sergeant Lampton and the others. The ground around Lampton's sangar was pock-marked with shell holes and the structure itself had been partially damaged by an explosion. Tom and Bill were still cleaning the weapons that had been clogged up with falling soil and dust. They both looked exhausted.

'Bloody marvellous,' Tom said. 'I cleaned these weapons at Um al Gwarif, I cleaned them again at the Mahazair Pools, I cleaned them when we climbed up to here, and then, after that fucking attack, I had to clean them again. Gravel, sand and dust spewing in every time a shell hit. A right fucking misery!'

'At least it wasn't your guts spewing out,' Bill said philosophically. 'Count your blessings, I say.'

'So what's happening, boss?' Ricketts asked.

'We're marching to Jibjat,' Lampton replied.

'Six kilometres west with all our gear in the heat of the noonday sun. Mad dogs and Englishmen.'

'Terrific,' Tom said. 'More sand, dust and other shit. More cleaning of weapons. Absolutely terrific.'

'This bothers you?' Lampton asked.

'It gets on my fucking wick.'

'You're still on probation,' Lampton said. 'If you don't like it, pack it in.'

'What?'

'I think you heard me, Trooper.'

'Jesus, boss, I didn't mean . . .'

'Don't take anything for granted,' Lampton said, 'just because you've been badged. All you people are on one year's probation, so never forget it.'

'Forget every word I uttered,' Tom said. 'Just wipe it out of your mind. OK, boss, what's the rope?'

'The rope is six kilometres long and it takes us to Jibjat. Do you walk or stay here?'

'I walk, boss. I'm on my feet already. I'm raring to go.'

'Then let's go,' Lampton said.

Impressed by Lampton's deceptively gentle demolition job on Purvis, Ricketts and the others helped to destroy the sangar, taking it apart stone by painful stone, as they had just done with their own; then they picked up their heavy loads and took their position in the spectacular gathering of some 800 men, broken up into dozens of extended, snake-like lines, stretching down the eastern hill, across the airstrip, then up the lower slopes of the western hill. All of them were wearing camouflaged clothing, with the *firqats* half hiding their faces in their wind-blown *shemaghs* and looking all the more fearsome by so doing. When everything was in order, a series of hand signals came down the line and the men moved out.

There was no talking. The various lines stretched out a long way, over the western hill, but the only noise was the jangling of kit and weapons hanging from webbing. At first the air was cool, but the sun was rising fast, and before long, as the last men crossed the hill, the heat made itself felt. Ricketts wiped sweat from his face; he swatted flies and mosquitoes. Though physically uncomfortable, he felt oddly at one with the great column of men snaking down the hillside, towards the flatland where the Jibjat airstrip lay. He knew that the *adoo* would be there, waiting for them, ready to fight, but even that thought filled him with a kind of wonder, rather than fear.

The march did not take long and soon the airstrip came into view in the distance, enclosed in a great horseshoe of high, rocky terrain, where the *adoo* were almost certainly entrenched. Immediately, as if communicating with body language, a subtle change came over the hundreds of marching men as they instinctively became more tense and watchful. They moved slightly away from one another, spreading out across the desert plain, until they were covering the broad area leading up to the rocky bottleneck leading to the airstrip. All of this was accomplished without a word.

Then the first shots rang out. Surprisingly, they were single shots from Kalashnikov rifles, fired by the *adoo* with unerring accuracy to pick off some of the SAF troops up front and perhaps demoralize the others. Some men fell, but the others kept marching, first walking as before, picking up speed, then gradually breaking into a run as they raced for the bottleneck. More shots rang out and more SAF troops fell, then a distant thudding sound indicated that mortars had just been fired.

The first explosions erupted on a wide arc where the troops were advancing, ripping up the ground between them and sending up a screen of boiling sand and smoke. The men at the head of the column disappeared into this as the *adoo* opened up with their machine-guns.

Green tracer illuminated the murk, exploding in silvery flashes, and making jagged, spitting lines in the sand that sent some of the advancing troops into convulsions before jerking violently backwards. The other troops continued to race into the turmoil as the medics ran to and fro, crouched low, bravely tending to the wounded, the dying and the dead.

'What the fuck are those bastards firing?' Gumboot asked, 'that can reach us from the far side of that airstrip?'

'Twelve-point-seven-millimetre Shpagin heavy machine-guns,' Lampton said as they all gradually broke into a trot. 'They can outrange anything we have, so we'll have to get a lot closer before returning their fire. Come on, lads, pick your feet up.'

Ricketts and his team tried to run as best they could while carrying the separate parts of the dismantled GPMG. For Ricketts it was hell, with the legs of the tripod biting into his neck and chest, but eventually he found himself in the thick of the smoke-filled, spewing sand, where the mortar shells and heavy machine-gun fire were causing most havoc. Here the other men advancing through the gloom were no more than shadows.

'Christ!' Andrew said, running beside him, 'I can't see a damned thing.'

Ricketts almost fell, one foot slipping into a shell hole, but Andrew grabbed him by the shoulder and tugged him upright, then pushed him ahead. Gumboot was there beside him, his face streaked with sand and sweat, running beside Tom and Bill – a trio of ghosts. The mortar shells were still exploding, making the sand roar and swirl about them, and green tracer zipped through the air with a vicious, spitting sound.

Suddenly, from the gloom of the swirling sand, they plunged back into daylight. For a moment it was dazzling, seeming brighter than it really was, but then, when Ricketts managed to adjust to it, he saw that the bottleneck leading to the airstrip had been blocked with a barricade of trees and barbed wire. Then he saw the *adoo* retreating across the airstrip, firing on the move, and gradually scattering up the rocky slopes beyond, where they could hide behind boulders.

'We should be in range!' Lampton shouted. 'Set up the machine-gun!'

Relieved to be unburdened, Ricketts dropped to his knees and, with Andrew's assistance, set up the GPMG. Once it was on place on its heavy tripod, he closed the top cover on a belt of 200 rounds and Andrew hammered out a test burst of 50. He then slipped the hinge-clip off the foresight of the barrel, took the foresight blade between his thumb and forefinger and screwed it up into position. After replacing the hinge-clip, he again took up his firing position, index finger on the trigger and thumb behind the pistol grip, so as not to accidentally move the gun with the natural pull of his fingers. Then, with Ricketts feeding in the belts, he started pouring fire into the hills where the *adoo* were sheltering.

It was difficult to tell what effect Andrew was having personally as by now the other SAF machine-gunners were also peppering the hill and the mortar crews were laying down a barrage that soon covered the whole area in smoke. The *adoo*, however, were in retreat, moving back up the hill, allowing the SAS demolitions team, led by the dour, red-headed Corporal Alfie Lloyd, to race across to the bottleneck to begin the task of blowing away the trees and barbed wire blocking the way to the airstrip. They were given covering fire, not only by the many machine-guns, but by a fusillade of fire from the 7.62mm FN rifles of the SAF, *firqat* and Baluchi troops now massed on both sides of the barricade.

With Ricketts feeding in the belts and Gumboot acting as observer, Andrew kept hammering away with his GPMG, helping to force the *adoo* back up the slopes of the western hill and over its rim. Meanwhile, Jock was in constant touch with the Head Sheds, who soon relayed the information that the barricade was about to be blown up.

By this time most of the *adoo* appeared to be well up the western hill, clearly retreating back over the rim, out of range of the SAF guns, so the machine-gun fire gradually tailed off. Andrew also stopped firing. Finally, the SAF rifles fell silent and the troops, realizing that the barricade was going to be destroyed, hastily retreated from both sides of it to crouch on the ground near the SAS.

Ricketts borrowed binoculars from Gumboot and scanned the rim of the western hill. Magnified by the binoculars, he could see the *adoo* clearly. Wearing jellabas, *shemaghs* and sandals, they were heavily burdened with webbing, ponchos, bandoliers of ammunition and long-bladed *kunjias*.

To Ricketts's untrained eye, the *adoo* looked just like the fearsome *firqats*. This could, he thought, cause some confusion in the future. Even as he watched through the binoculars, most of them stopped firing and retreated back up the hill, cradling their Kalashnikovs in their arms. Ricketts handed the binoculars back to Gumboot when the last of them were about to disappear over the rim of the hill.

The demolition men had completed their work and were retreating backwards, crouched low, uncoiling the detonation cord as they went. From where he was kneeling, Ricketts could clearly see the plastic explosives taped to the up-ended trees. The det cord, with one end fixed to blasting caps embedded in the explosive charges, was running out from the explosives to the roll being uncoiled by Alfie Lloyd. When he and his assistant had reached the detonator, Lloyd cut through the cord with scissors, expertly bared the wires with a pocket knife, fixed them to the electrical connectors on the detonator, then kneeled above the latter, resting his hands lightly on the plunger.

He scrutinized the barricade to ensure that no one was near it, then glanced at Major Greenaway, who was kneeling about ten yards to his right, beside RSM Worthington and a radio crew. When Greenaway raised and lowered his right hand, Lloyd pressed down on the plunger.

The noise emerged from what seemed like the bowels of the earth to explode with a deafening roar and spew out a mighty mushroom of soil, sand, dust and loose gravel. The trees were blown apart and burst into flames, raining back down through the boiling, dark smoke as a fountain of fire, falling into the murk some way to each side of the bottleneck and causing more dust to billow upwards.

The fading noise of the explosion was followed by another – the spine-chilling, macabre wailing of the excited *firqats*, rising eerily above the cheering and shouting of the SAF and Baluchi troops. As one man, they jumped to their feet and raced through the billowing smoke in the bottleneck, between the exploded, flaming trees, then spread out across the deserted airstrip, firing their weapons repeatedly in the air to announce their triumph.

Bemused by the furore, the SAS men followed them in.

13

Though the position had been taken, it had to be consolidated, a job beginning with the clearing of the airstrip, which was littered with spent shells and the debris of mortar and other explosions. As the runway had not been tarmacked, but was merely level ground cleared and flattened by human hand, the filling in of the few shell holes was relatively easy and completed by men from the Royal Electrical and Mechanical Engineers (REME), most of whom worked stripped to the waist in the boiling heat. The job was almost completed by noon, when the sun was a white ball in the azure sky.

As Major Greenaway well knew, the *adoo* 'retreat' was in fact merely part of a typical guerrilla strategy involving staying out of sight and harassing the enemy with sniper fire, mortar shells, and small, daring hit-and-run raids of the kind the SAS could only admire. These activities went on throughout the morning while the

REME teams filled in the shellholes and cleaned up the airstrip, to enable the planes to bring in more men, supplies and equipment, including some badly needed ground transport. Luckily, most of the mortar shells had fallen on the lower slopes of the western hill, well short of the runway, and the sniper fire, while causing the REME men to jump, also fell well short.

Nevertheless, knowing that small groups of *adoo* snipers would almost certainly sneak down the western slope to fire from behind rock outcrops, within range of the airstrip, the SAF commander, after consultation with Greenaway, sent some of his own teams to patrol the lower slopes.

By mid-afternoon, Ricketts, Andrew, Gumboot and Jock had built another sangar, on a hill due north of the airstrip. There, sitting on their bergens and drinking a brew-up, they were able to rest while observing the work going on below. When not sipping hot tea or surveying the activities around the airstrip, Andrew scribbled more poetry in his notebook.

'What the fuck are you writing about now?' Gumboot asked him.

'What's going on down there,' Andrew replied, not looking up from his notebook.

'How the hell can you write poetry about *that*?'

Gumboot asked. 'I thought poetry was all blue moons and posies.'

'It can be about anything, Gumboot. War and peace, love and hatred, the sound of church bells ringing out over Hereford, the smell of your old socks.'

'One word about my old socks,' Gumboot said, 'and I'll have you for libel.' He glanced down the hill. 'Nice to see those REMF sods doing some work at last.' 'REMF', not to be confused with 'REME', meant rear echelon motherfuckers, which is why Gumboot used it with such relish. 'They've been sitting on their arses since we got here, so let them sweat for a change.'

'They work for their keep,' Ricketts said, 'making life more pleasant for us. So stop complaining.'

Glancing down the hill, he saw that Sergeant Lampton, whose friendship he had already come to value, was again sharing a sangar with Tom and Bill. Obviously, the sergeant was making sure that all of his probationers were in sight and easy to reach. Below, around the airstrip, the REME were opening a lot of packing crates and removing some of the tools they would need to construct the camp. More tools and the heavier equipment would be brought in on the planes.

'I wonder how Greaves was,' Jock asked,

removing his shirt and wiping the sweat off his white skin. 'He looked a right bloody mess.'

'He was scorched by the blast,' Ricketts said, 'and peppered with shrapnel. He won't walk for a long time.'

'A lot of SAF troops copped it as well,' Jock said, putting his shirt on again to ensure that his white skin did not burn, 'and they won't walk at all.'

'No, I guess they won't, Jock. They were pretty fearless, weren't they?'

'Aye, they were.'

'Not like those fucking *firqats*,' Gumboot said. 'Ready to lay down their arms at the least excuse.'

'That's not cowardice,' Andrew said, slipping his notebook into his breast pocket. 'They never stop fighting because they're scared. They either do it on an impulse because of something else that's come up – say, they feel offended by something – or for religious reasons, such as Ramadan.'

'I don't give a shit about their reasons,' Gumboot said. 'My concern is that the bastards aren't dependable. That's what has *me* worried.'

'You're always worried about something, Gumboot. A regular bundle of anxieties, you are. Go ask the doc for some Valium.'

'A couple of pints would do me better,' Gumboot sighed.

'Sweat and suffer,' Ricketts said, then contented himself with looking down the hill, at all the work going on far below in the increasing light and heat.

As the REME finished clearing the airstrip and organized the building of defensive 'hedgehog' emplacements and sangars, as well as marking out the separate areas of the camp they would create here, Alfie Lloyd's demolitions team blew up the last obstructions placed by the *adoo* between the airstrip and the western hill, leaving the way clear for a full-scale advance at a later date.

Remarkably, the first of the resup aircraft were flying in before last light. The very first Skyvan brought in the keenly awaited marquee tent to be used as a mess, a proper field kitchen, supplies of compo food, water and mobile electrical generators to be used for general lighting around the camp and for recharging radio, vehicle and other batteries. The second Skyvan brought in dismantled 25-pounders, for emplacement in the 'hedgehogs'. The three Hueys and single Sikorski helicopter began the lengthy process of landing more men while the first Skyvans took out the wounded and dead, including Greaves, for casevac from RAF Salalah back to England.

All of this was observed by Ricketts and his mates from their sangar halfway up the northern slopes. During the morning and afternoon, they were baking in the heat and, as usual, driven mad by flies and mosquitoes, but as last light came the air started turning cold, reminding them that they were in for an uncomfortable night. They were, however, heartened to see the mess tent being put up by the REME while the kitchen staff unloaded the equipment brought in on a Skyvan. By last light, the kitchen was in operation and men were queuing up at the mess tent, now brightly illuminated inside with lamps lit by the mobile generators.

Tired of living off brew-up and high-calorie rations from his survival belt, Jock contacted Lampton on his PRC 319 radio. 'We have a bit of a problem up here, boss,' he said while gazing at the sangar further down the hill, where he could actually see Lampton with his own radio.

'Hear you loud and clear, Trooper. What's the problem?'

'An acute shortage of high-calorie rations, boss, hand in hand with the desperate yearning for a decent meal.'

'I still hear you loud and clear, but this sangar has no kitchen, so why are you bothering me, Trooper?'

Jock grinned at Ricketts. 'Seems to us, boss,

that there's bright lights and a healthy queue down in that mess tent.'

'I have eyeball contact, Trooper, and *can* confirm. In fact, I'm just on my way down there myself to tag onto that queue. Any more problems, Trooper?'

'A little problem of permission, boss, given that we're on watch. Not complaining, mind you.'

Lampton broke down and laughed, then spoke through a wave of static. 'OK, Trooper, you win. The Regiment respects persistence. Two men have to be on watch at any given time, which means one man at a time down in the mess. My recommendation's for a Chinese parliament to decide. Either that or toss a coin if you've got one. Over and out.'

Not having a coin between them, they scratched a head on a small, flat stone and flipped it three times, with the first loser being condemned to go downhill last, the next loser second to last, the third loser second and the winner first. Ricketts, however, rigged it so that Jock could have first go as a reward for getting on the blower.

While Jock was in the mess tent below, making up for his two days of enforced dieting, Ricketts and the other two carefully shook out their gear, then rolled out two sleeping bags in the sangar. Only two of them would be allowed to sleep at any one time, with the other two keeping watch together, with each one ensuring that the other was still awake.

Waiting for Jock's return, Gumboot huddled up in the sangar, protected by the wall of stones, and had a smoke. Ricketts and Andrew, their weapons resting lightly on the wall on either side of the GPMG, kept watch in all directions. After the heat of the day, the night was bitterly cold.

When Jock returned, Gumboot hurried down-hill and Jock took Andrew's place on watch, letting the latter huddle down behind the wall to warm himself and have a cigarette. Andrew went down next, with Gumboot taking Ricketts's place beside Jock, allowing Ricketts to huddle beneath the wall, out of the biting wind. By the time Andrew returned, Ricketts was feeling a lot warmer and hurried down the hill to the mess, in the mood to eat.

After the dark and cold of the hill, the mess tent seemed brilliantly illuminated, warm and inviting. It was, indeed, packed and noisy, with everyone in a good mood, and Ricketts relished his compo sausages, mashed potatoes, green peas and baked beans, followed by apple pie and hot custard. He was there for forty minutes, had a good talk with some other troopers, then reluctantly climbed back up the hill to relieve Jock on watch. The men then took turns at watch, or stag, two on, two off, until first light.

Sleep, when it came, was constantly interrupted as the *adoo*, still pursuing their guerrilla tactics, fired their rifles and mortars at irregular intervals throughout the night.

The resup flights had also continued throughout the night and by first light the following day Skyvans, Caribou transport planes and helicopters had lifted in defence stores and ordnance; full and empty oil drums, the latter to be used to build defensive walls; water and rations; jeeps, trucks, Saladin armoured cars; donkeys for carrying heavy loads on mountain patrols; and even live goats to be killed, cooked and eaten by the *firqats*.

'Talk about special privileges!' Gumboot complained. 'We eat compo rations and those A-rabs get live goats for their fucking couscous. A diabolical liberty!'

'The food's part of their religion as well,' Andrew explained, 'which is why they get those so-called special privileges.'

'How come religious people get everything and we sinners get nothing?'

'It's the same back in England,' Andrew said. 'The same in America. Religion excuses every damn thing.'

'Still, it's a fucking liberty. We get sausage and beans and they get bloody couscous.'

'Would you actually eat couscous, Gumboot?'

'Are you fucking crazy? That shit's for the birds!'

'There you are, then.'

'Never mind what I'll eat or not, Andrew. It's the fucking *principle*, mate!'

'Couscous for breakfast, dinner and tea,' Jock said, 'must be a wonderful, stomach-wrenching experience.'

'You'd be farting like a whale with gastritis,' Gumboot warned him. 'Stay well away from it, mate!'

From their vantage point high on the northern hill, Ricketts and Andrew, in particular, found it fascinating to observe with what speed and efficiency the base camp was built around the original, largely featureless airstrip. Artillery positions consisting of 40-gallon-drum hedgehogs were built on all four sides of the runway and manned with 25-pounders and Browning 0.5in heavy machine-guns, the latter having a range of 1400 metres and a firing rate of up to 500 rounds per minute. Sangars were placed at regular intervals between the hedgehogs and armed with Browning 0.3in medium machineguns – range 900 metres and 400–500 RPM – and Carl Gustav 84mm rocket launchers. Other sangars were equipped with the same MMGs, but had 81mm mortars instead of the rocket launchers. The combination of heavily armed hedgehogs and sangars formed a natural defensive perimeter around the base camp.

The work was completed by lunchtime the second day. By late afternoon, marquees and bivouacs were sprouting all over the area, with many of the latter in two sets of three lines, making an accommodation area for the SAS, SAF and Baluchi troopers, each with their individual lines. The two sets of tents were divided by an area of flat land to be used as a football pitch and general recreation area. Portable showers and chemical toilets were raised near the tents. An artificial wall was created from piled Burmails to protect the rows of bivouacs from the four LZs specially cleared for the helicopters. South of the airstrip, near the cleared bottleneck, was a fenced-in armoured car parking area. Above it, near the eastern hill, were the officers' tent lines and toilets, the mess tent, and a captured enemy personnel, or CEP, tent. North of the airstrip, obliquely below Ricketts's sangar, were marquees used as the rations, equipment and ammunition stores. Located well away from those and the accommodations areas, in order to avoid the smell, was a donkey handler's tent with fenced-in area for the donkeys, plus a similar area for the goats and goatherds. As they were not bothered by the smell and indeed had sole use of the goats as a source of food, the *firqats* had their own camp, located near the base of the western hill. From there they could constantly patrol the hill with the support of SAF troops.

By last light on the second day, the camp was a thriving community, with goats and donkeys braying; SAF and Baluchi troops being noisily and rigorously drilled by their officers; REMFs hammering, drilling and shouting instructions; SAS troops playing football on the new pitch; *firqat* members slaughtering a squealing goat, draining it of blood, skinning it, and cooking it over an open fire; jeeps and Saladin armoured cars roaring and rattling all over the place; helicopters ascending and descending from their four LZs; and Skyvans and Caribou transports continuing to land and take off on the runway, bringing in more supplies and taking out what was no longer required.

All of this took place while *adoo* mortar shells and FN rifle fire continued to tear up the earth on the slopes above the western perimeter.

Shortly after the last of the four-man team in Ricketts's sangar had returned from the mess tent, Sergeant Lampton came up the hill at the crouch to squat beside them and tell them what was happening.

'The force is being split into two fighting units, or fire groups,' he told them. 'The first, called the Eastern Group, will be tasked with probing deeper into the eastern area. As the *adoo* beyond the western hill are gathered around the Ain watering-hole, the second group, the Western Group, of which you'll be part, are going to start clearing them out tomorrow. This sangar, including the machine-gun, will be taken over by some other troopers while you lot rejoin Purvis and Raglan to gain experience in close-contact mountain fighting, under my guidance. We move out at . . .'

'First light,' Andrew interrupted him.

Lampton grinned. 'You're obviously learning, Trooper. Now have a good night.'

The sergeant slithered his way back down the hill, to the sangar he was sharing with Tom and Bill.

Later, close to midnight, the *adoo* released their most sustained volley of fire since surrendering the airstrip. From Ricketts's position in the sangar, he could see the eerily beautiful, gracefully arching, green tracer gliding out from the pitch-black western hill, picking up speed as it curved down towards the airstrip, then exploding either on the ground or spending itself in silvery bursts in the darkness above the many tents of the new camp. It was a magical sight he would never forget.

Though he did not know it then, it was the beginning of five days of bloody fighting.

14

The intermittent rifle and mortar fire of the night allowed Ricketts and his mates very little sleep. Struggling awake at first light, when Gumboot and Jock were still on watch, he felt sleepless, cold and full of faint aches and pains. Sitting upright and rubbing the sleep from his eyes, he glanced over the sangar wall just as another mortar explosion shook the lower slopes of the western hill, sending a column of sand, soil and smoke into the pearly-grey air.

'Christ,' he said, 'I feel shattered.'

'Aye,' Jock agreed, a cigarette dangling from his lips as he leaned on the wall beside the GPMG with his M16 rifle resting across the stones. 'Me and Gumboot, we've just been saying the same thing. What a fucking night!'

'Right!' said Gumboot. 'Fireworks all night long. Just to keep our eyes open. I can't remember when I last had a good sleep. My eyes feel like lead.'

Andrew, who had been sleeping beside Ricketts, groaned and also sat upright. 'Shit,' he said, 'I feel terrible.'

Jock and Gumboot laughed. 'You better get used to it,' Jock said. 'I don't think we'll get much rest today – nor tonight for that matter. Here come our replacements.'

Ricketts glanced over the wall again and saw the new four-man team making their way laboriously up the steep hill. A similar group was already at Lampton's sangar, replacing the sergeant, Tom and Bill, who were presently making their way downhill. Pale sunlight was falling on the dry earth, streaking the grey light with silvery striations that heralded the heat. On the western hill, there was no sign of the *adoo*, who had been firing on and off all night and were continuing to do so. Most of them were hidden behind the rim of the hill, but others, Ricketts suspected, were sniping from behind the slope overlooking the camp – the slope that he and the others would soon be climbing. The thought filled him with a slight, healthy tension that would stand him in good stead.

The replacement team finally reached the sangar. Exchanging greetings, they sounded breathless.

'That's some climb,' one of them said.

'Sure is,' Andrew replied, rolling up one of the

two sleeping bags and stuffing it back into his bergen. 'It clears out the lungs, right?'

'Right,' the replacement replied.

Jock and Gumboot were enthusiastically humping their bergens onto their shoulders as Ricketts rolled up his own sleeping bag and stuffed it into his bergen. This done, he hoisted the bergen onto his shoulder, picked up his SLR and stepped out of the sangar.

'Good luck,' he said to the four men as they took over the sangar.

'And to you,' one of them said. 'You're the ones who'll need it.'

After waving goodbye, Ricketts scrambled with the others down the hill and into the newly erected camp. The rich aroma of boiled lamb and spices reached them from the *firqats'* camp near the base of the western hill, where the Arabs, all wearing their jellabas and *shemaghs*, were kneeling around an enormous communal pot piled high with couscous, which they were scooping into their mouths with their fingers.

Gumboot screwed his face up in disgust, then held his nose as they passed the goats. But by the time they reached the mess tent, they were well out of range of the smell and were greeted instead with the welcoming aroma of bacon and eggs.

Entering the tent, they found it packed, the men queuing up along the servery and then taking their plates to the trestle tables. After the usual bullshit with the cook, they had a slap-up fried breakfast washed down with hot tea, their weapons stacked up around them, then made their way to the ammunition store, where they had to collect spare ammo and meet Lampton. The sergeant was waiting for them when they arrived.

'Morning, lads. Got a good night's sleep, did you?'

'Wonderful!' Jock said. 'Slept all of ten minutes.'

'Now we're bright-eyed and bushy-tailed,' Gumboot added, 'and rarin' to go.'

They had to join another queue to pick up their spare weapons, which included, as well as their standard-issue Browning high-power handguns and SLR or M16 rifles, Heckler & Koch MP5 9mm sub-machine-guns and, for some of them, 7.62mm Lee Enfield sniper rifles. Tom and Bill were given an M-72 LAW, and others, Ricketts noticed, were collecting 51mm and 81mm mortars with base plate, tripod and shells – heavy loads to be humping up that hill in the increasing heat of the morning. To increase the load even more, each group was carrying at least one PRC 319. It would not be an easy day.

The men then joined the many others grouping together near the hedgehog by the base of the western hill. The group, known as the Western Group, tasked with clearing the eastern slope of the western hill, consisted of the majority of B Squadron and G Squadron 22 SAS, the Firqat Al Asifat, the Firqat Salahadeen and the Baluch Askars. Being organized by British officers, notably Major Greenaway, they were surprisingly indifferent to the mortar explosions erupting at irregular intervals on the hill. In fact, the explosions were all fairly high up, out of range, as were the occasional *adoo* rifle shots.

'OK,' Lampton said to Ricketts and the others, 'you men will be with me, coming up behind that group of *firqats* gathering over there.' He indicated the Arab fighters with a nod of his head. Bristling with bandoliers, webbing and weapons, looking as fierce as usual, they were listening intently to Dead-eye Dick as he gave them instructions. With his L42A1 7.62mm bolt-action Lee Enfield sniper rifle slung across his back, his webbing bristling with ten-round box magazines and L2A2 steel-cased fragmentation grenades, a Browning high-power handgun holstered on his hip, and his two knives – a *kunjias* and a Fairburn-Sykes commando knife – sheathed on the belt around his waist, Parker looked every bit as fearful as his *firqat* comrades.

'Shit,' Gumboot whispered, 'are we going with *him*?'

'Yep,' Lampton said, grinning.

'That bastard terrifies me,' big Andrew said. 'I'm not sure I like this.'

'He's a good man,' Lampton said. 'Good tracker, great sniper. He's a good man to have in your area, so you should be thankful you've got him. Whoops! Here comes the briefing.'

Standing on a wooden crate, so that everyone could see him, Major Greenaway gave a short speech, saying that their ultimate task was to clear the Ain watering-hole and take command of the whole plateau, but that before that they would have to take the western hill and thus ensure the safety of the Jibjat airstrip.

'Therefore,' he said, 'you will climb the hill in your separate groups, flushing out the *adoo* where you find them and hopefully taking some prisoners for interrogation. It's anticipated that you'll be on the rim of the hill by last light. From that vantage point, you'll direct the fire of the 25-pounders onto the *adoo* positions on the other side. We will keep this barrage going all night.'

'There goes our sleep,' Gumboot whispered.

'At first light,' Greenaway continued, 'you will make your way down the other side, pushing the *adoo* back to the watering-hole. Once that's been accomplished, you'll all regroup at the bottom of the hill in preparation for the final assault on the watering-hole and ultimately the Wadi Dharbat, where most of the *adoo* are entrenched. Any questions?' The major looked around him, but saw only heads shaking from side to side. 'No? Good. You may now proceed with all speed.'

The first of the SAF, *firqat* and Baluchi troops were already starting up the hill when Greenaway jumped down off his box and headed back to his HQ tent in the camp, accompanied by RSM Worthington. At the same time Sergeant Parker walked up to Lampton, nodded at him, then turned to Ricketts and the others, to study them with icy grey eyes.

'We go up the hill together,' he said finally, 'but well spread out, with me and the *firqats* out front, you lot behind us. We advance at the crouch, from one outcrop to another, never standing fully upright and making sure that we're never fully exposed for more than a few seconds.' His voice was soft, almost a whisper, with hardly any timbre or intonation; not a comforting sound. 'The *adoo* can see through rocks, use their eyes like periscopes, and have eyes in the back of their heads as well. You stand up and you'll get a bullet through *your* head and fucking deserve it. Don't panic up there. Don't shoot the wrong people. On the other hand, if anything moves, don't take too long to decide. Keep your eyes to the front and to the ground, because there might be land-mines. OK, let's go.'

Ricketts and the others glanced uneasily at one another, then followed Lampton up the lower slopes, behind Parker and the *firqats*. At first the climb was easy, on a gentle incline, but before long the rise was much steeper, the ground underfoot rougher. As Parker had instructed them – and as he and the Arabs were doing now – they spread well apart and made the climb on the crouch, darting from one outcrop to another, trying desperately not to slip on the loose stones and slide back down the hill. A backbreaking activity, sending pains through every muscle, it was made even more difficult by the flies and mosquitoes that buzzed frantically around their lips and eyes. The rising heat only made it worse and they were soon bathed in sweat.

Tying his *shemagh* around his mouth to keep out the flies, Ricketts glanced in both directions and saw the many other SAF, *firqat*, Baluchi and SAS troops, totalling over two hundred, advancing up the lower slopes by the same painfully slow yet effective method. Glancing over his shoulder, he saw the camp spread out below, an apparently chaotic collection of tents, hedgehogs and sangars spread around the airstrip and four helicopter LZs on baking earth covered with wind-blown sand. Reflected heat rose up from the ground, distorting the shape of solid objects, making them appear to bend and wobble. The men down there, whether walking or driving, were indistinguishable from their shadows, which also shifted and changed into bizarre shapes in the shimmering heat.

Ricketts looked to the front again just as rifle shots rang out and an SAF soldier was slammed backwards to the ground, then rolled down the hill in a cloud of dust. Even as those around him were crouching low behind outcrops and raising their weapons to return the fire, more bullets kicked up the sand around them and ricocheted off the rocks. The return fire was quick, exploding from many SAF weapons, turning the hill above into an inferno of angrily spitting, jagged lines of sand.

When it died away, however, there was still no sign of the *adoo* who had killed the SAF soldier.

'The phantom enemy,' Andrew whispered. 'Now we know why they call them that.'

'Move further apart, you two!' Lampton snapped, waving his left hand.

'Yes, boss,' Andrew replied, again putting a good distance between himself and Ricketts, crouched low, then dashing across open space to drop down behind another outcrop.

Parker and the *firqats* were up ahead, moving

in a north-south arc, away from the main assault force. More *adoo* sniper fire rang out from even higher above, causing sand to fly all around the *firqats*. Parker's head popped up and down as he checked the source of the fire, then he leaned out from the sheltering rocks, taking aim with his Lee Enfield, and snapped up three quick shots in a row before pressing himself back into the rock.

A man came rolling down the hill, limbs akimbo, jellaba flapping and dust billowing up around him, only stopping when he crashed into a large rock near the *firqats*. He was still alive, groaning and gargling, his body twitching, but one of the Arabs darted across to where he lay, rolled him over and slit his throat with a *kunjias*.

'Christ!' Gumboot said.

'Keep moving!' Parker shouted, waving them on with one hand and running uphill, crouched low, as the Arab stripped the dead man of his bandolier and weapons, then divided them among the other tribesmen. Ignoring them, Lampton urged Ricketts and the others up the hill, still crouching low and darting from rock to rock as more bullets thudded into the ground around them or ricocheted off the surrounding rocks.

So it went on for a couple of hours – the men jumping up and down, scurrying from rock to rock, dropping low and then jumping up briefly to fire a shot. Another body rolled down the hill. A *firqat* was hit, and threw up his arms, his robes billowing behind him, and jerked back to land on the slope with a sickening thud.

Jock had the PRC 319 and called up the medics. While he was doing so, a mortar shell exploded nearby, creating a spiralling column of smoke and sand. The roar of the explosion was followed by screaming in Arabic and another fusillade of fire from the advancing SAF soldiers, though to what effect no one knew.

The *adoo* were still hard to find. They popped up and down from behind the rocks above, jel-labas fluttering, eyes wide above their *shemaghs*, only to disappear and reappear somewhere else, picking off the SAF troops with daunting accuracy. And yet they were in retreat, backing gradually up the hill, and as more of them were hit and tumbled down in clouds of dust, the remainder, of whom there were clearly many, retreated up the hill even faster.

Progress was being made, but it was not easy, and by noon, when the hill was like a furnace, with heat shimmering up off the scorched, dusty rocks and even the insects seemingly dazed, Ricketts, feeling as tired as the others looked, was grateful to take five. In fact, the break lasted for an hour, allowing the men to rest up and eat some high-calorie rations, washing them down with water; but then the PRC 319s started crackling and hissing, relaying the order to move, and the men climbed laboriously to their feet and started the whole thing again.

They had another four hours in hell, burning up in its cruel heat, tormented by flies and mosquitoes, by scorpions and centipedes underfoot, while being picked up by the hawk-eyed *adoo* snipers and, on the odd occasion – when the *adoo* heavy gun teams forgot the danger to their own men – by the erupting soil and flying shrapnel of mortar explosions. More bodies littered the hillside and were carried away by the sweating medics, but gradually, as the afternoon passed into evening, and the heat died down, they began to force the *adoo* back over the hill. By now Parker had led his group well away from the main assault force and was moving towards the summit of the hill in the planned north-south arc.

Ricketts saw the levelling summit and the featureless sky beyond; he was exhilarated enough to forget to stay low when he made his next zigzagging run to another outcrop. An *adoo* sniper fired at him and the bullet, after hitting the stock of his SLR and making the weapon spin out of his hand, ricocheted off the rock he had quickly dropped behind, spraying his face with pulverized stone and temporarily blinding him.

Blinking to clear his eyes, Ricketts saw the *adoo*

sniper running at him, striped jellaba billowing in the breeze, his FN rifle in one hand, a *kunjias* in the other, the latter reflecting the sunlight as the man held it high.

The SLR was out of reach, still lying where it had fallen, so Ricketts quickly tore his Browning handgun from its holster and swung it up into the two-handed firing position: in line with the centre of his body, locking his arms, his free hand holding the firing hand, and with equal pressure between thumb and fingers as he pressed gently, precisely on the trigger.

A double-tap – two shots fired in quick succession – and the Arab was stopped, staggering back, dropping his knife, then turning aside, as if trying to be polite, before falling face-down in the dirt.

Ricketts lowered the handgun and took a deep breath. After checking that the man was dead, he holstered the weapon, picked up his SLR, noted with relief that it was OK, and then followed the other men up to the summit.

It was a rocky plateau, scorched white by the sun, stretching out quite a distance before falling away again. Beyond the slope of the eastern side of the plateau, the desert stretched out for what seemed to be for ever, though it was merely that the horizon was virtually invisible in the heat haze. The sun, however, was going down, sinking behind the men, casting its light on the hill they had just climbed. In front of them, to the east, the fading light was gradually, magically, bringing the lost horizon back into view, at least before extinguishing it again in the darkness of night.

The Ain watering-hole and Wadi Dharbat, Ricketts surmised, were at the bottom of the eastern hill of the plateau, now safely out of sight. Perhaps for this reason, and knowing that they were to dig in here for the night, in order to call down support from the 25-pounders in the hedgehogs in Jibjat, the men were shaking off their bergens and lowering themselves to the ground, looking forward to slaking their thirst or having a smoke.

They were instantly disillusioned when Lampton and Parker came storming back from the eastern slopes, the latter saying in his soft-voiced, deadly way, 'What the hell do you troopers think you're doing?'

'Well, Sarge,' Jock began, 'we just thought . . .'

'That you'd won the fucking hill? You've won nothing, Trooper. You sit here on your arse, having a cigarette, and the *adoo* will come back over that ridge and blow the shit out of you. Now get back on your feet and start picking up rocks and build yourselves a sangar big enough to take all of you and that LAW. Is that understood?'

'Yes, boss!' Andrew said, loud and clear.

'Good,' Parker replied and started turning away.

'Just one thing, boss,' Gumboot said, looking surprisingly clear-eyed.

Parker turned back to face him. 'Yes, Trooper?'

'While we're building our sangar, boss, what will your *firqats* be doing?'

Parker stared steadily at Gumboot, burning up with an inner fire, then smiled, almost in admiration, and said, 'A fair enough question, Trooper. They'll be building another sangar, about a thousand metres from here, to the south, and I'll be with them, keeping in touch with the 319. While you, with Sergeant Lampton's help, call in grid references for the 25-pounders in Jibjat, we'll be foraging out over that eastern hill with the intention of bringing back a prisoner. Any problem, Trooper?'

'With you all the way, boss. No sweat.'

'Glad to hear that. Start building.'

As Parker walked away to rejoin his Arab fighters, Gumboot let his breath out in a lengthy sigh of relief.

'I've got to hand it to you,' Andrew said, 'you've got nerves of steel, Gumboot.'

'I thought I had,' Gumboot replied, 'until that cunt looked at me.'

Lampton laughed. He had been standing just

behind them. They all stared at him until he quietened down and said, 'Sorry, lads, but you're all being paranoid. Dead-eye's perfectly normal. Come on, let's build the sangar.'

As usual, they tore the rocks out of the earth with their bare hands and piled them one on top of the other to create a natural wall. It was a semicircle, the open end to the rear, the curved wall overlooking the plateau and the vast, star-filled darkness beyond it. They placed their weapons around the wall, rolled out their sleeping bags – not for sleeping but to sit on – then checked their small-scale maps and button compasses by the light of pencil torches and, combining their readings with eyeball recces of the landscape, radioed back approximate calibrations to the big-gun teams in Jibjat.

All along the great length of the plateau overlooking the Wadi Dharbat and the Ain watering-hole, other OP teams were doing the same. Within minutes, they heard the dull, distant thumping of the big guns, followed seconds later by shells whistling overhead, then by the sound of explosions on the lower slopes of the eastern hill and the flatland beyond, with luck including the wadi and the watering-hole. Though only being targeted on a broad, general front, the big guns could not fail to do extensive damage before the assault force moved out, which would not be until first light the following day.

'Fucking hell,' Bill said, covering his ears, 'that's one hell of a noise.'

'No beauty sleep tonight,' Tom added. 'We'll move out deaf and dumb.'

'Better deaf and dumb than dead,' said Gumboot. 'Which is what a lot of those poor fuckers are going to be before first light dawns.'

'Dead right,' Andrew said.

When first light came, many hours later, the sky beyond the sunlit plateau was dark with drifting sand, dust and smoke. It was billowing up from the explosions far below, but the men could not see those. They broke the sangar up stone by stone, then began their long march down to the burning plain.

15

They had not gone very far across the plateau when they saw Parker coming up over the rim, holding his Lee Enfield sniper rifle across his chest. He was followed by his fierce-looking Arabs, who were dragging an *adoo* prisoner between them. The latter's ankles had been tethered with a short length of rope that made it difficult for him to walk. It ran up to his wrists, which were bound in front of him, thus making any other kind of movement just as difficult as walking.

Lampton stopped in front of them, letting Ricketts get a good look at the prisoner. The man had a gaunt, hungry face and darkly blazing, defiant eyes.

'Ah,' Lampton said, 'I see you had a good night.' Parker just nodded in agreement. 'Any other contact down there?' Lampton asked him.

'We terminated a few,' Parker said in his oddly disturbing manner, 'and saw that there's a lot of them. They were scattered all over the eastern hill, though I think they're making their way back down to regroup at the watering-hole. I heard a lot of trucks coming and going during the night, accompanied by the sounds of digging, so I think they were laying mines in the flatland leading up to the watering-hole.'

'Damn!' Lampton said softly. 'What about our 25-pounders? Did they do any good?'

'Yep. I think the shelling was what forced the *adoo* back down the hill. They were on the move while we were foraging about there. We terminated a few more before first light, taking them out with knives so as not to be noticed, then grabbed this prisoner for the green slime. I'm going to hand him over for questioning, then I'll come back and join you.'

'The green slime have set up in a tent in Jibjat, so you'll have to take him all the way back.'

'I'll send him with an escort of troopers and be with you in no time.'

'OK, Dead-eye. Excellent.' Lampton raised his right hand and waved it in a forward motion, indicating that the men should follow him.

They marched past Parker's group, heading across the plateau, towards where the ground sloped away to form the eastern hill. Once at the slope, they found themselves looking down on the broad stretch of desert leading to the watering-hole and the Wadi Dharbat. Both the lower slopes of the hill and the flatland at the bottom were covered in a pall of smoke and a lazily drifting cloud of sand and dust. The hill was strewn with rocks and littered with black shell holes. No dead bodies were visible.

'The *adoo* have removed their dead,' Lampton said. 'I respect them for that.'

Glancing in both directions, they saw other SF troops, including SAS, also crossing the plateau, weapons at the ready, and beginning their careful descent of the hill towards the flat plain. Ricketts saw the glint of water between curtains of smoke – the Ain watering-hole – surrounded by what looked like another horseshoe-shaped series of hills and ridges, forming a natural, presently ghostly amphitheatre.

'That's where the *adoo* will be waiting for us,' he said.

'Yes,' Lampton said. 'Let's go.'

Moving parallel with the others, they continued downhill, stepping carefully around the shell holes and scorched, blackened boulders while keeping their eyes peeled for signs of mines or *adoo* snipers.

The big guns were still firing at regular intervals as the men advanced. However, given new calibrations from the forward observers, they were firing on a much higher trajectory, dropping the shells on the flatland just short of the watering-hole, trying to force the *adoo* out of there and into the wadi.

Shells were exploding all over the flatland as the assault force made its way down the hillside. With no big guns of their own, the *adoo* were withholding fire until their targets were within range of their 81mm mortars, Shpagin heavy machine-guns, GPMGs and Katushka 122mm recoilless rocket launchers.

This was not something to contemplate with much enthusiasm, but Ricketts took some comfort from the softening-up barrage of the 25-pounders and assumed that his friends were doing the same.

There were no *adoo* snipers on the hill, nor were land-mines encountered. The men reached the bottom in thirty minutes and kept marching across the flat desert plain. In no time at all they left the bright sunlight of morning and found themselves advancing into the dense smoke and drifting dust created by the exploding shells. It was always nerve-racking in the smoke, with visibility reduced to zero, impossible to see land-mines or booby-traps and easy to become disorientated.

The range of the *adoo*'s Katushkas, Ricketts knew, was almost 11,000 metres, which meant that another five minutes' marching would put him and the other SAF troops within range. He was worrying about this and the possibility of mines when he saw a jagged flash well ahead, accompanied by an explosion, a dreadful scream of agony, the clashing of different voices bawling warnings or commands, some in Arabic, others in English, then the gradual grinding to a halt of the men around him.

'Land-mine!' someone bellowed up ahead. 'Don't move! Land-mine!' That fearful call was followed by, 'Medic!'

Pierced by a bolt of fear that had to be contained, Ricketts froze where he was, but glanced about him, seeing the others as barely recognizable, shadowy forms in the murk, all standing dead still just like him. Their presence was a comfort, though a residual fear nagged at him, and he knew that he would not have felt so bad had it happened in clear light. As it was, trapped in the fog of smoke, spiralling sand and drifting dust, his feeling of helplessness was greatly increased. But it was lucky at least, he told himself, that they were still out of range of the enemy's Katushka rocket launchers.

'What the fuck happens now?' Gumboot asked, standing beside Ricketts and talking just to hear the sound of a human voice.

'The SAF have a team of mine detectors spread out across the plain at the head of the column,'

Lampton said, positioned ahead of them and glancing back over his shoulder. 'They'll have to advance slowly, checking for more mines, and the assault force will break up into as many single files as are required to follow the men with the mine detectors. When I move, get into single file behind me and follow in my footsteps. Don't deviate one inch.'

They had to wait a long time, with the smoke still drifting around them, listening to the continuing barrage of the big guns. Eventually, the shelling stopped, the gun crews having been alerted to the plight of the assault force, and the sand and dust gradually settled down. The smoke started thinning, too, letting Ricketts see farther ahead. Just as it cleared enough to let him glimpse the front of the column, which was on the move again, the men directly in front of him started moving too.

When Lampton raised and lowered his right hand, indicating 'Forward march', Ricketts and the others fell in behind him, but in single file, as ordered. Lampton moved very slowly, as if barefoot on broken glass, and Ricketts was careful to follow precisely in the footprints left in the sand.

Eventually, after ten minutes that seemed more like ten hours, the smoke cleared, and Ricketts saw the hundreds of men, advancing slowly, carefully in numerous long lines. Each man was following the footsteps of the man ahead, all tailing back from the men with the mine detectors, spread out across the front of the column over a distance of about a quarter mile.

It was a tortuous advance that would leave them sitting ducks for the *adoo* when they got within range. For that very reason the column was stopped again and instructions sent down the lines via the PRC 319s.

Lampton had been listening to his call from Major Greenaway and now he handed the phone back to Jock, in charge of the radio.

'The CO says we can't advance this way, at this speed, once we're within range of the *adoo* guns – we'd just become sitting ducks. So he's asked for the Skyvans to come over and clear the area with Burmail bombs. In the meantime, we wait.'

'Can we sit down?' Gumboot asked.

'I think that's safe enough,' Lampton said. 'Your arse is probably no wider than your big feet. Just don't move left or right.'

'Ha, ha,' Gumboot said.

Desperate for a rest, the men sat on the ground and saw many of the other soldiers doing the same, though some felt it more prudent to stay standing.

By now the sun was up, blazing out of a clear blue sky, and with the dispersal of the smoke, sand and dust, it felt hotter than ever. Even more irksome, the flies and mosquitoes returned, materializing out of the ether, buzzing, whining and dive-bombing in a feeding frenzy brought on by sweat and blood. A lot of the men put on dark glasses and covered their mouths with *shemaghs*, but the swarm just flew or crawled under them to get at their eyes and mouths.

The men baked in the sun, became nauseous in the heat, swatted and slapped to no avail, cursed and groaned while they waited. It was not a long wait, but it seemed like an eternity. Eventually, to their relief, the Skyvans were heard flying over the hill dividing the plain from Jibjat. When the three aircraft came into view, many of the men cheered.

In the brilliant sunlight, Ricketts could clearly see the rocky amphitheatre surrounding three sides of the watering-hole presently being held by the *adoo*. He judged it to be approximately 15,000 metres away, which was too far for him to pick out individual details, but left only 4000 metres between the column and the firing range of the *adoo*'s Katushka rocket launchers.

That danger was yet to come. For the moment, Ricketts took a great deal of pleasure from watching the Skyvans fly directly above him and on to the mined desert plain just ahead of the column. They were flying very low. Once they had passed overhead he saw that the rear cargo holds were open, with men standing in them, dangerously close to the edge, but behind the stacked Burmails. They simply pushed the oil drums out, probably sliding them off rollers. Ricketts saw the drums clearly, falling down through the sky, one after the other, with the Schermuly flares burning like firelighters on each side of them. They appeared to fall slowly, almost gliding, but that was an illusion.

When the first drum hit the ground, it bounced like a football, then exploded with a thunderous clap and became a boiling mass of brilliant flame spewing over the plain. The other Burmails did likewise, one after the other, some bouncing crazily before exploding, others seeming to burst open at once, and many catching fire from the great waves of flame that were boiling and leaping into one another to form an immense wall of fire capped by black, oily smoke.

As intended, the explosions set off the landmines in another series of explosions covering most of the area between the stalled assault force and the entrance to the rocky amphitheatre surrounding the watering-hole. Mines not touched directly by the Burmails were set off by exploding mines in a domino effect that created a fantastic, awesome spectacle of boiling flame, billowing smoke and widly swirling columns of sand, dust and loose gravel. It went on and on, a constant roaring and burning so intense that the watching troopers felt relatively cool when the flames finally died away.

'Jesus Christ!' exclaimed Andrew, too stunned to get out his notebook.

'Fucking A!' Gumboot added.

A few minutes later the desert floor was smouldering, with isolated flames – the results of gaseous burning created by the oil – spiralling a few feet above the ground before sailing away like yellow threads and finally becoming mere wisps of smoke that also gradually disappeared. When nothing but the thinning smoke remained, the column moved on.

The *adoo* opened fire with their Katushka rocket launchers the instant the column had advanced another 5000 metres. As this placed most of the men within range of the rockets, the explosions erupted in their midst, causing devastation and death, with some soldiers being thrown up and smashed back to the ground in turbulent clouds of flame-filled smoke.

Instead of trying to take cover, since there was none available, the men started running, determined to get to the watering-hole before they were slaughtered. When the first of them reached the natural entrance, the *adoo* opened fire with a combination of Kalashnikovs, FN sniper rifles and GPMGs, cutting down even more troopers. This forced them to scatter north and south, to both sides of the amphitheatre, from where they could continue their advance by alternately hiding behind, and scrambling over, the rocks.

Three members of a four-man SAS GPMG team, trailing the SAF troops during the advance into the minefield, had been killed by the first mine explosion. The fourth man, now squatting on the ground beside his GPMG, was clearly in shock.

'Arrange to have that man sent back,' Lampton said to the medic on the scene. Then he turned to Ricketts and said, 'You lot are back on your original job. Pick up that GPMG and find a spot on those rocks.'

'Right, boss,' Ricketts said.

Andrew picked up the GPMG, using a sling to support it in a position conducive to firing from the hip. When Ricketts had slung the tripod onto his shoulders, helped by Gumboot, they all hiked it up to the rocky south wall of the opening, into the horseshoe-shaped area surrounding the watering-hole. They were soon joined by Major Greenaway, RSM Worthington and the redoubtable Sergeant Parker.

While Greenaway immersed himself in a briefing huddle with his RSM and two sergeants, the mortar and GPMG teams set up their weapons, aiming them across the watering-hole at the high ground opposite, which was hidden by thick thorn bushes and therefore ideal for a waiting enemy. The watering-hole itself was about 650 yards away, at the far end of the U-shape formed by the legs of the horseshoe, which opened up towards the SAF forces, including the SAS.

Lampton left the briefing huddle and returned to tell his men what was happening.

'The mortar teams and SAF will jointly hold this position,' he said, 'giving fire support to three SAF action groups and the Firqat Khalid bin Waalid. Those four groups, plus an SAS platoon coming up on the right flank, will advance tactically into the bowl and secure the watering-hole.'

Nodding his understanding, Ricketts opened the steel tripod and placed it firmly in the dusty ground. He then levelled the cradle and locked it. After centralizing the deflection and elevation drums, he fitted the GPMG, pushing the front mounting pin home until the locking stud clicked into position. Gumboot then flicked up the rear sight-leaf and set it on the 300-metre graduation, laying the sight on to a rocky outcrop on the tree line by use of the deflection and elevation drums. Finally, they sandbagged the legs and rechecked the sight. The gun was ready for firing.

The men then realized that they were in an excellently concealed firing position, with panoramic views of the whole area.

'Fucking perfect,' Gumboot said. 'We can see the whole show from here.'

'And it looks like it's just starting,' Andrew replied, pointing with his forefinger to where the *firqats*, about to move down the rocky gradient into the horseshoe, had stopped to have what appeared to be an excited argument with the SAF officers.

'Oh, oh!' Bill murmured, spitting on the rock between his knees.

'They've gone on strike,' Tom said drily.

Parker and Lampton hurried up to the group of *firqats* and SAF, listened to both sides of the argument, offered their suggestions, then nodded at each other, as if in agreement. Parker then went back to give his situation report, or sit rep, to Greenaway, while Lampton returned to his men to do the same.

'Having an argument, were they?' Gumboot asked sceptically.

'A Chinese parliament,' Lampton replied diplomatically. 'The *firqats* wanted us to mortar the high ground and fry the tree line with a mixed-fruit pudding before the action groups moved off.'

'A *what*?' Tom asked.

'A mixed-fruit pudding,' Lampton repeated impatiently, before remembering that his men were probationers. 'Two high-explosive shells to one white phosphorus, fired by mortar.'

'Ah!' Tom said. 'Right!'

'However,' Lampton continued, 'the actual action groups, the SAF, insisted that time is running out and that every *adoo* in the area will be homing in on the water-hole if they, the SAF action groups, don't make an immediate move to secure it.'

'Even before the mortars have time to get their bearings,' Gumboot said.

'Correct.'

'So what's the result?' Tom asked impatiently.

'We've vetoed the mixed-fruit pudding, but the *firqats* and action groups are moving off immediately on the basis that the mortar crew have already monitored the high ground and have possible *adoo* firing points on their plotter board.'

The men glanced over Lampton's shoulder to observe that the *firqats* were indeed already heading down into the horseshoe, followed by the SAF troops.

'Fucking terrific logic,' Gumboot said, as if he couldn't believe his own ears.

Lampton grinned. 'It's *their* logic, Gumboot. Now get ready to cover them.'

Ricketts closed the top cover of the GPMG on a belt of 200 rounds. Andrew then cocked the action and put the safety catch on 'Fire'. Gumboot scanned the area with binoculars while Jock, his jaws working on chewing gum, kept his ear to the radio.

The area around the watering-hole seemed unnaturally quiet. Dust was blowing across the wet sand surrounding the pool. The sun was blazing down on the white rocks and erasing the shadows. Flies clustered like bunches of black grapes over mounds of old excrement. The heat was fierce and oppressive.

The heavily armed *firqats* advanced in an extended line, holding their rifles out from their bodies, preparing to fire from the hip.

Suddenly, about halfway to the watering-hole, they fell one after the other belly-down on the ground, from where they frantically waved the action groups forward.

'What the hell . . .' Lampton looked confused. 'That's not what they're supposed to do. They're *supposed* to go all the way, because it's their watering-hole and tribal area. The SAF were letting them take that position to boost their morale. What the . . .?'

'They're on strike,' Gumboot said, sounding satisfied.

The SAF action groups were advancing through

the lines of prone *firqats* when the high-velocity rounds of the *adoo* suddenly shattered the silence.

The ground erupted around the SAS with fire from Kalashnikov AK-47s, RPD light machine-guns, and at least one Shpagin heavy machine-gun. A stream of green tracer floated towards the SAS mortar and GPMG positions, then whipped above their heads at incredible speed, only to expend itself harmlessly at the burn-out point of 1100 metres, well behind them.

'There!' Gumboot shouted, lowering his binoculars and pointing towards a cloud of blue smoke rising from the top of some thorn bushes on the high ground beyond the watering-hole. 'That's the heavy machine-gun! Range – 400 metres. A hundred metres right to take it out – behind those rocks, over there. Rapid fire! *Now*!'

Andrew obliged, firing off a lengthy burst, his ears ringing from the clamour, and saw his purplish tracer blending with the green tracer of the *adoo*.

'Too high,' Gumboot said. 'Reduce the elevation.'

Ricketts did this by unlocking the elevation drum and giving it a quick tweak downwards. This time, when Andrew fired, the tracer penetrated the thorn bushes where the smoke was rising, tearing them apart and making pieces of dust and stone fly off the rocks right beneath them. When the debris of the hit had settled down, the Shpagin machine-gun was silent.

The SAS mortars now began firing as well, with phosphorus rounds adding to the noisy spectacle and more silvery flashes exploding in the thorn bushes. Between the SAS mortars and GPMG, the thorn bushes along the high ground were blown apart and most of the *adoo*'s heavy guns were silenced.

Just then, however, as the SAS platoon was advancing on the exposed right flank, expecting cover from the advancing *firqats*, the latter stopped dead and started screaming in unison at the SAF troops just behind them. Incredibly, as *adoo* tracers whipped past them and bullets stitched the ground around them, the *firqats* engaged in a heated argument with the SAF troops, thus preventing the advance of the latter and allowing a group of *adoo* to come down off the high ground, take up positions behind rock outcrops and ambush the SAS troops advancing on the right flank.

'Christ!' Lampton exclaimed. 'I don't believe it!'

'That's the second group to go on strike,' Gumboot said as Lampton snatched the phone from Jock and got in touch with Sergeant Parker, who was crouched low beside a trooper with a PRC 319, near the arguing *firqats*. 'Lampton here! What the hell's going on?' Before Parker could answer, Lampton lowered the phone and bawled over his shoulder: 'Give them covering fire!'

Even as Lampton returned his attention to the radio, Andrew fired into the high ground on the right flank where the *adoo* were advancing on the SAS troops, some of whom were already wounded or dead.

'Randall's hit!' the radio crackled. 'McGuffin also hit! We're . . .'

The urgent voice was cut off when an exploding fragmentation grenade, thrown by one of the advancing *adoo*, blew the radio apart and flipped the operator onto his back. The assailant was then thrown onto his back when Parker took him out with a single shot from his 7.62mm Lee Enfield. Parker then jumped up and ran to help the platoon on the right flank, firing from the hip as he advanced, only stopping long enough to hurl a grenade into the midst of the *adoo* moving towards them. The explosion blew the group apart, flipping some of the men over, leaving others to stagger blindly to and fro, most soaked in blood, some blinded by shrapnel, all of them easy marks for the SAF riflemen, who soon picked them off.

The SAS platoon, almost lost in the ambush, then rushed forward, up to the high ground, joined by Parker. As they did so, Ricketts and the other probationers supported Andrew's noisy, murderous GPMG fire with their SLRs and M16s, followed by Tom and Bill's mortar. In doing so, they killed many *adoo* and forced the others back up the hill. The SAS action group then took control of the lower slopes and the SAF, having settled their argument with the *firqats*, continued their steady advance on the watering-hole.

'Day's work done,' Andrew said, releasing the trigger of the GPMG and waving the others into silence. 'I think we're home and dry, man.'

Even as he spoke, one of the SAS troopers threw a smoke grenade into the area chosen as a casevac point, marking it for the incoming chopper with a cloud of green smoke. Called in via a PRC 319, the casevac Huey soon arrived to land in a cloud of dust. Mere minutes later it was taking off with the casualties, some wounded, others dead. It headed back to the field surgical theatre of RAF Salalah without interference from the *adoo*, who had melted away.

'They've gone into the Wadi Dharbat,' Lampton said, 'adjacent to here. That's where we'll be going next.'

While the *adoo* were out of sight, the SAS

action groups, now followed by the *firqats* instead of being led by them, secured the watering-hole. Lampton then led Ricketts and the rest of the probationers in, saying, 'I'm really proud of you men. You've all done a great job.'

The whole area was littered with the evidence of battle – piles of 7.62mm shells and empty cases, bloodstained bandoliers and blood trails, pieces of flesh and torn clothing – but no bodies. The *adoo* had dragged them away. The air stank of burnt flesh, phosphorus and cordite. It also stank with human excrement over which bloated flies were relentlessly, frantically hovering, oblivious to the battle that had raged about them.

After a short break, Lampton made Ricketts and the other probationers take up new positions on the high ground above the watering-hole. Even up this high, they could smell the phosphorus and cordite from below, but after building another sangar, they broke out their hexamine blocks, lit the lightweight stove, boiled water from their water bottles and had a well earned brew-up.

'Why did the *firqats* stop advancing?' Bill asked when Sergeant Lampton dropped in for a chat.

'The *firqats* and the SAF soldiers despise each other,' Lampton explained, 'and when one of the latter accused the former of advancing too slowly, all hell broke loose. Thereafter, the *firqats* refused to lead the way into the watering-hole. It was as simple as that.'

'Well, fuck me with a bargepole,' Gumboot said, 'if that doesn't take the cake.'

'I wouldn't want to do that,' Andrew said, 'because you just might enjoy it. Pass the brew, Gumboot.'

Already the Skyvans were coming in with the resups, dropping such luxuries as mail from home, cigarettes, water, ammunition and fresh rations. The men drank their tea, swatting the flies away, ducking the mosquitoes and waiting patiently on the high ground, beneath the blazing sun, for the next phase of the bloody operation. When another Skyvan flew overhead, their friend, Corporal Whistler, stripped to the waist, waved at them from the rear cargo hold. He was pretty safe up there.

16

During a night and day spent in their sangars on the high ground, the men learnt that it was still not safe to wander about freely, as the *adoo*, though located mainly in the nearby Wadi Dharbat, were sending snipers back to do as much damage as possible. Therefore, though Lampton's blooded probationers spent most of that time in their sangar, other troopers were patrolling the high ground, flushing out the snipers, checking for land-mines, and generally securing the area. While this was largely successful, the snipers were persistent and no matter how many were caught or killed, others came in to replace them. Sporadic firing therefore continued unabated, with the odd soldier being wounded and no one able to properly rest up.

'Fucking bastards,' Bill said. 'They're just doing it to keep us awake and get us exhausted, the miserable shits.'

'Clever shits,' Andrew corrected him. 'They

don't have our fire-power – they're particularly lacking in heavy, long-range guns – so they fight us the only way they know how: with guerrilla tactics. You have to admire them.'

'Admire them! Are you fucking joking? They're just a bunch of miserable A-rabs, costing us sleep. They're murderous, mindless bastards, is all.'

'They're tenacious,' Ricketts said. 'Great marksmen. Courageous, as well. I agree with Andrew.'

'They're not courageous,' Gumboot said. 'They're just a bunch of fanatics. Brainwashed by the fucking commies in Aden and sent back here like zombies. They don't have the sense to think of dying; it means nothing to 'em. I don't call that courage.'

'You're just a racist,' Tom said.

'That's right, I'm a racist. I hate you bastards from the Midlands. I figure you're as mad as the *adoo* and should be put down at birth.'

Ricketts glanced down the hill at the sandy area around the watering-hole. It was now filled with back-up troops from Jibjat – SAF, Baluchi, *firqats* and SAS – with tents, sangars and hedgehogs springing up rapidly. Braying donkeys were being unloaded from a couple of Bedfords and passed on to the gathering *firqats*, who would use them for carrying heavy supplies up into the high hills. When Ricketts looked to the west, through the entrance to the amphitheatre, he saw Land Rovers and Saladin armoured cars creating billowing clouds of dust as they drove down the eastern hill, then across the sun-whitened plain pock-marked with black shell holes.

'The *adoo* aren't mad,' Andrew insisted, resting his notebook on his lap and tapping his teeth with his ball-pen, and pursing his lips, trying to think of something to write. 'They just think different from us. Born and bred in the desert, in a merciless environment, they view matters of life and death in a way we can't possibly imagine.'

'What he means,' Gumboot said, 'when you get past the fancy words, is that they'd slit your throat as soon as look at you. They don't think about death, you see.'

'We think about death in the West Midlands,' Tom said. 'The weather's so merciless, you don't want to get out of bed — you want to stay in the womb. You think of death a lot, then.'

Gumboot rolled his eyes. 'You hear that?' he said to Andrew. 'We have our home-brewed A-rabs in England and they're all from the Midlands. Mad as fucking hatters, and even think they're white men. What do you *do* up there,' he asked Tom, 'when you're not thinking about dying?'

'Lots of nice pubs where I live, ten-pin

bowling, darts. I've never missed a West Bromwich Albion game. Plus social evenings with old mates from the glassworks. Quite a nice life, really.'

'I'm breathless just thinking about it,' Gumboot said. 'What about you?'

Bill shrugged. 'Pretty varied life, really. The Four Furnaces, the Commercial, the Albion, the High Oak, the Elephant and Castle, the Fish, the Rose and Crown, and the Miners' Welfare Club on Commonside. Course on Wednesdays I'd play dominoes and on Tuesdays cribbage. Like Tom says, quite a nice life.'

'You hear that?' Gumboot said, addressing the distracted Andrew. 'The only time these bastards get out of the pubs is when they're called back to Hereford.'

'Wrong,' Andrew replied, jotting words down in his notebook. 'They play dominoes, cribbage and ten-pin bowling. They go to football matches. They check the weather and crawl into bed and think of death as they throw up. How *they* can look down on the Arabs, I just can't imagine!'

'Go fuck yourselves,' Bill said.

Flashing his teeth in a big smile, Andrew lowered his pen and glanced over the sangar wall at the watering-hole. The sun was blazing down, reflecting off the water, as the Land Rovers and

Saladin armoured cars drove into the clearing, the first of them braking to a halt near the braying donkeys, which were being herded away by the *firqats*.

'Donkeys and armoured cars,' Andrew said dreamily. 'The past and the future, the old and the new. We are straddling both worlds here.'

'The donkeys and the *firqats* are perfectly matched,' Gumboot said. 'I don't have to tell you why.'

Glancing down the hill, Ricketts saw Sergeant Lampton disengaging himself from a group of SAS men, including Major Greenaway, RSM Worthington and Sergeant Parker, who were grouped near the arriving Land Rovers and Saladin armoured cars.

'The Land Rovers and Saladins are coming in,' Ricketts said, 'to lend their support to the planned advance on the Wadi Dharbat.'

'I wish I was in a Saladin,' Andrew said, 'well protected by all that armour and those 76mm QF cannons, instead of having to do all this hiking, being shot at by snipers.'

'I'm not too sure I'd agree,' Ricketts answered thoughtfully. 'I like being in the open. I don't fancy the idea of being cooped up in an armoured car. They aren't all that easy to get out of. If they catch fire, you've had it. If a shell penetrates them, the shrapnel flies like crazy around the interior, slashing and burning everything inside. Even the turrets are a kind of trap. I keep remembering those poor bastards in the Saladin outside Um al Gwarif. They were probably killed because they couldn't get out in time. So, you know, there's certain advantages in being a foot soldier, out in the open. At least you can cut and run.'

'True enough,' Andrew said.

Glancing down again, Ricketts saw that Lampton was making his way laboriously up the hill, obviously heading for the sangar to impart the latest sit rep. Below him, on the level ground between the watering-hole and the parked Land Rovers and Saladins, Greenaway and Worthington were still in deep discussion with the granite-faced Parker.

'What do we know about Dead-eye Dick?' Ricketts asked, directing his question at the whole group.

'That he's fucking mad,' Gumboot said.

'A good soldier,' Bill added.

'A born killer if ever I saw one,' Jock said as he distractedly fiddled with the dials on his PRC 319. 'That bastard slits throats for breakfast.'

'He's pretty bloody frightening,' Tom said, glancing automatically down the hill to where Parker was. 'I mean, he doesn't seem normal.'

'He isn't normal,' Andrew said. 'He used to be,

but he isn't any more. He was in the Telok Anson swamp and that changed him for all time.'

Everyone stared intently at Andrew. 'The Telok Anson swamp?' Ricketts asked eventually.

Andrew nodded. 'Malaya, 1958,' he said. 'I got this from Sergeant Lampton. Parker was only twenty at the time, a probationer like us, and he was sent with D Squadron to Malaya. It was pretty hairy out there, always living in the jungle, but Parker proved to be a natural soldier and even better tracker. For that reason, in the spring of 1958, he was parachuted with two troops from D Squadron into the Telok Anson swamp, to go up against a bunch of CTs, or communist terrorists, led by the notorious Ah Hoi, nicknamed "Baby Killer". That swamp was a nightmare, the terrorists were even worse, and Parker was there for ten days, practically living in the water with the leeches and snakes. When he came out, he was changed for all time. Whatever happened in there, it obviously wasn't pleasant, and it certainly did something drastic to Parker. When he emerged, so Lampton said, he was no longer a baby-faced probationer – in fact, quite the opposite. He was . . .' Andrew shrugged, unable to find the correct words. 'The man we all know and revere. The one who makes us shit bricks.'

'And piss our pants,' Gumboot said.

'Right on, brother. Right on!'

Lampton, breathing heavily, had finally reached the sangar and gratefully sat on the wall, trying to get his breath back.

'Some climb,' he said.

'Piece of piss,' Gumboot replied. 'We run up and down it every five minutes without missing a breath. Of course, *we're* just probationers.'

Lampton grinned. 'I must be past it, Gumboot. I'm glad to know, however, that you're all fit enough to take what's coming.'

'What's that?' Jock asked, looking suspicious.

'The CO's decided that we've been here long enough, so he's going to deploy our forces on the plateau. We, the SAS, will be divided into two separate groups, each one being accompanied by *firqats* . . .'

'Oh, no!' Gumboot exclaimed.

'. . . with orders to advance down the western and eastern sides of the Wadi Dharbat, taking out the *adoo*. How does that grab you, gentlemen?'

'I'd rather let an *adoo* cut my throat,' Gumboot said, 'than depend on them fucking *firqats*. Come to think of it, if we're going to depend on them, we might as well cut our own throats and be done with it.'

Lampton grinned again. 'You exaggerate, Gumboot. I'm sure that now, with the differences between the *firqats* and the SAF troops resolved, you'll have no trouble at all with the former.'

'Very nicely put, boss. It shows you're educated. It also shows you're more optimistic than I am. Thanks, but no, thanks.'

'Orders are orders, Gumboot.'

'Please don't remind me, boss.'

'You have thirty minutes to break up the sangar and get down to the watering-hole.'

'Hear you loud and clear, boss.' When Lampton had slithered back down the hill, Gumboot raised his hands imploringly and looked to the heavens. 'What have we done to deserve this? What sin can be that bad?'

Andrew laughed, stood up, and placed his large hand on Gumboot's shoulder. 'It was the sin of being born, Gumboot. Now let's break up this sangar.'

They destroyed the sangar in no time, now expert at it, then moved carefully down the hill, spread well apart, keeping their eyes and ears alert for *adoo* snipers. Reaching the bottom without mishap, they joined the large group of other troops, including the *firqats*, gathered around Major Greenaway, who was standing up in the front of a Land Rover as if on a stage.

'As you doubtless know,' he said, 'the *adoo* are now entrenched in the Wadi Dharbat, eight kilometres' march from here. However, the high ground between here and that wadi is crawling with snipers. Your task will be to advance down the eastern and western sides of the wadi, taking out the *adoo* you encounter en route and, when you reach the wadi, clearing the remaining *adoo* off the plateau for good. For this purpose, you'll be divided into two groups – the Eastern Group and the Western Group – with each taking the side designated by its title. Both groups will be supported by members of the Firqat Khalid bin Waalid, who know the terrain and should be invaluable as scouts, trackers and support fighters. Your respective platoon leaders will now tell you what group you're in. We move out in thirty minutes, at noon precisely. Good luck, men.'

'Nice to know that the *firqats* are going to be our scouts,' Gumboot whispered sardonically to Ricketts. 'That means we'll be back in Um al Gwarif for supper – by accident, naturally.'

Nevertheless, despite Gumboot's doubts, they were assigned to the Eastern Group and moved out at noon on the dot, accompanied by a large contingent of *firqats*, who were at least, so Ricketts noted with relief, under the supervision of Dead-eye Dick Parker.

Spreading well apart, they clambered up the high ground, moving at the crouch, as Parker had taught them, and darting from one outcrop to another, leaving themselves exposed as little as possible. For this particular march, Andrew had discarded the GPMG tripod and was supporting it with the aid of a sling, intending to fire it from the hip. Tom and Bill were still struggling with the mortar components. Jock had the PRC 319 as well as his standard-issue weapons. Gumboot only had his standard-issue weapons, including an M16 semi-automatic rifle, and a pair of binoculars. Ricketts, relieved of the heavy, awkward GPMG tripod, was feeling as free as a bird with only his normal kit and weapons, including the SLR.

He was actually humming to himself when the first shot rang out and Tom jerked like a puppet on a string, dropping his M16, his left leg buckling, the weight of the mortar barrel pulling him back as the pain struck and he cried out. The men were falling low even as he hit the ground in a cloud of dust.

'Sniper 45 degrees east!' Lampton bawled from out front as Tom let out a piercing, long drawn-out scream and hammered the ground beside him with his clenched fist. Ricketts fired his SLR. Gumboot and Lampton let rip with their M16s, making the rocks above spit chipped stone and dust. 'I'm hit!' Tom yelled, getting his breath back after the scream. 'Oh, Jesus! The bastard!' Jock was speaking into the radio, calling for a medic, even as the sniper readjusted his aim and put a bullet through Tom's forehead, splitting his skull in two and turning it into a pomegranate with pieces of bone washed out on the blood that splashed over the sand.

'Purvis hit!' Jock screamed into his mike as the others kept firing and Parker appeared out of nowhere, higher up than the sniper. He rose up from behind a rock, taking aim with his Lee Enfield, fired a shot and then waved his right hand to send one of the *firqats* down. The latter ran down at the crouch, forcing the others to stop shooting, and stopped at the outcrop from which the *adoo* sniper had been firing. Having examined Parker's quarry, who must have been shot through the back, the *firqat* straightened up and waved his hand, indicating that the sniper was dead. Parker waved back, then turned away and hurried on up the hill, followed by the *firqat*.

'Tom is dead,' Andrew said.

'I can't bear to look,' Jock told him.

'Christ, what a mess,' Gumboot whispered. 'What the fuck do we do with him?'

Lampton slithered back down the hill, his feet kicking up clouds of dust. After glancing at Tom's bloody, shattered head, he asked, 'Did you call a medic, Jock?'

'Yes, boss. He's on his way up.'

'Then there's nothing more we can do here, so let's get moving, lads.' Lampton started turning away, then noticed Bill. He was staring at his friend, too shocked to speak, trying to reconcile that dreadful image of smashed bone and blood with the man he had shared a lot of good times with. Though trying, he failed.

'Get the fuck up,' Lampton snapped, grabbing Bill by the shoulder and tugging him to his feet. 'We haven't time to sit here brooding. Now get up that hill, Trooper.' Bill just stared at him. 'Go!' Lampton screamed. Bill twitched as if slapped, blinked, glanced about him, said, 'Sorry, boss,' and turned away. He crouched low, his M16 at the ready, and hurried on up the slope.

'Gumboot!' Lampton snapped.

'Yes, boss.'

'Take that mortar tube off Purvis and then stick close to Raglan.'

'Shit, boss, he's all covered in . . .'

'Do it, Gumboot. Don't argue.'

'Right, boss. Will do.' Taking a deep breath and trying not to look, Gumboot rolled Tom over to get at his webbing and unstrap the mortar tube. When he had done so, which he only managed with great difficulty, avoiding the sight of the dead man's head, he strapped the tube to his own bergen, took another deep breath, then hurried to catch up with the others, falling in close to Bill. Though the latter's eyes were wet with tears, he was looking determined.

'He'll survive,' Gumboot whispered as he crouched behind a rock. Then he jumped up and zigzagged, crouching low, to another position.

The others were doing the same, zigzagging uphill, hiding behind rocks and leaping out and then dropping low again. They heard sporadic gunshots all around them – other snipers, more victims – but they managed to reach the crest of the hill without further incident.

It was only when they were starting down the other side that the *adoo* appeared. They might even have heard the gunshots first, but no one could be sure of that. It was a whole group of *adoo*, on a ridge just up ahead, about twenty yards away, some firing from behind the rocks, others advancing down the left flank. One of them jumped up in full view to swing his arm and hurl something.

'*Hand grenade!*' Lampton bellowed.

Ricketts turned away, pressing his back to a rock, lowering his head between his raised knees and covering his face with his hands. Nevertheless, he heard the explosion, felt the heat of the blast, choked as sand and dust rained on him, and felt gravel pepper him.

He turned around before it subsided, raising

his SLR, letting the barrel rest on the rock as he took aim and fired through the swirling, dust-filled smoke. Gumboot and Jock were doing the same, both covered in sand and dust, while Parker and Lampton covered the left flank with a hail of withering fire.

The *adoo* advance was stopped, some scattering, others falling, a few looking indecisive, the bullets turning the rocks and ground around them into a maelstrom of spitting dust and flying stones. The indecisive ones died in that turmoil, but one of them, having broken away from the others, suddenly bore down on Bill. His left hand had been shot off and was pumping blood like a fountain, but his right hand was holding a *kunjias*, which he was raising on high. Concentrating on the front, Bill failed to see his attacker. Ricketts saw him and fired a lengthy burst that made him dance like a demented doll, falling backwards and flipping over a rock and hitting the ground in a cloud of dust, his *kunjias* clanging noisily on the stones near his sandalled feet.

Ricketts looked to the front again, where the other *adoo* were still firing. He saw Parker jumping up to throw a grenade, ducking again as it sailed through the air and dropped behind the ridge. The explosion uprooted thorn bushes and sent up a column of soil and sand, and was followed immediately by the screaming of the wounded *adoo*.

Parker was up and running before the clamour died away, closely followed by his Arabs, some of whom were releasing macabre wailings and swinging their glittering *kunjias*. Ricketts gave them covering fire, aiming left of their advance, while the men beside him aimed to the right. Parker went up and over the rocks, jumping down on the *adoo*, firing his Lee Enfield from the hip as he disappeared over the other side, followed again by his *firqats*.

Ricketts saw a *firqat* swinging his gleaming *kunjias*, then jumped up and ran for the ridge without thinking about it. He reached the rim and stopped there for a short moment, aiming down with his SLR, but not firing immediately.

Parker was crouching low, holding his rifle in one hand, lunging upwards with his Fairburn-Sykes knife, to stab it into the stomach of an *adoo* who was trying to strangle him.

The *firqats*, still wailing in their strange, unearthly way, were slashing at the other *adoo*, whose jellabas were in tatters and soaked with blood.

Momentarily muddling the *adoo* with the *firqats*, Ricketts stood there, not firing, completely exposed, until he was pushed over the other side by someone behind him. Landing on his feet, he saw an Arab coming at him, swinging a *kunjias*, and he fired a burst that almost cut him in two. The *adoo's* upper half leant forward – like an Oriental gentleman being very polite – as blood burst from his belly and mouth. His eyes, above the bloodsoaked *shemagh*, rolled up in their sockets.

Ricketts stepped back to let his victim fall forward, then Gumboot and Andrew jumped down beside him, followed almost instantly by Lampton and Jock, both of whom glanced left and right, at the dead, bloody *adoo*.

'Oh, man!' Andrew exclaimed softly.

'A real slaughterhouse,' Gumboot said.

'Damned lucky you're still in one piece,' Jock told them, 'let alone standing upright.'

'Serves the bastards right,' Bill said, 'for what they did to my mate.'

As they stood there, glancing about them, seeing clouds of flies feasting, more *firqats* were gathering along the ridge to wail in triumph and shout blessings for this victory. Then, realizing that no more could be done here, they jumped down and raced on towards the Wadi Dharbat, following the redoubtable Parker, whose OGs, Ricketts noticed, were soaked in the blood of his *adoo* victims.

'What the hell are you all standing here for?' Lampton bawled. 'Let's head for the wadi!'

Shocked back to reality and instantly oblivious to the dead men lying about their feet, they all followed the sergeant away from the ridge and on to the eastern side of the Wadi Dharbat, where all hell was breaking loose.

17

They advanced on the Wadi Dharbat in the late afternoon, when the sun was going down in the west, casting long shadows and turning the white hills a mellow golden colour. Lampton was leading his own group, but Parker and his *firqats* were well ahead of him, the latter now confident with victory and keen to fight again. More troops were advancing along the west side of the wadi, strung out in long lines that ran from the lowland to the crest of the high ground, appearing from behind rocks, disappearing, then reappearing, the sound of gunfire a clear indication that they were meeting resistance. Lampton's group had seen nothing since leaving the ridge an hour ago, but the sound of gunshots up ahead, where Parker's Arab fighters were merely part of a larger SAF force, including SAF and Baluchis, was an indication that they, too, were having to flush out *adoo* snipers as they advanced.

'Take five!' Lampton shouted, raising his right hand to signal that they could stop.

Sighing with relief, Ricketts used a smoothly rounded rock as a chair while he wiped sweat from his face and drank awkwardly from his water bottle, having to hold his hand over the spout to keep the frantic flies and mosquitoes out. After screwing the cap back on and clipping the bottle back on his webbing, he slid a stick of chewing gum into his mouth, hoping to get rid of the taste of sand and dust.

Gumboot lit a cigarette, inhaled luxuriously, then pursed his lips and blew a few smoke rings.

'Well, Gumboot,' Andrew said, wiping sweat from his glistening black forehead with a hand-kerchief and grinning mischievously, 'you've got to hand it to Parker's *firqats* – they fought like demons back on that ridge and proved they had courage.'

Gumboot looked carefully at Andrew, not too sure of his grounds here. 'I never said they didn't have courage,' he replied defensively. 'I just said the fuckers weren't dependable and I stand by that.'

'Admit it, Gumboot, they're OK.'

'They may have been OK back on the ridge, but that doesn't make them dependable. All whooping and hollering when we took out the *adoo*, but I'd still like to see them in a tight spot. I wouldn't exactly sit back with a smoke, letting them get on with it, I can tell you that, mate.'

Ricketts noticed that Bill was sitting slightly apart from the others, blowing thin clouds of cigarette smoke and looking decidedly unhappy, still shocked by the death of his friend. Lampton, who had been keeping his eye on him, said, 'Are you OK?'

Bill just stared at him, as if not understanding.

'I asked if you were OK,' Lampton repeated.

'Sure. Why shouldn't I be?'

'I know that Tom came as a shock. It always is the first time.'

'Are you telling me it gets better, boss?'

'You get used to it,' Lampton said.

Bill snorted derisively. 'Right,' he said. 'You get used to it.' He inhaled and blew another thin stream of smoke. 'His head,' he said, as if talking to himself. 'I keep seeing his head. I never thought . . .' He trailed off into silence, glanced left and right, blinked, then inhaled and exhaled, trying to keep himself steady.

'That's a form of self-indulgence,' Lampton said, 'and we haven't time for it. Put all thought of Tom out of your mind and concentrate on the task at hand. If you don't, you could make a mistake and endanger us all. Is that understood?'

'I'm OK,' Bill said.

'Good. Glad to hear it.' Lampton was just about to stand up and wave them all forward when he heard a distant, familiar, hollow thudding sound. '*Mortars!*' he bawled and dropped into a crouch as the shells came whistling in from a great height.

The others either looked up automatically or threw themselves to the ground as the first of the explosions erupted about twenty feet away, hurling soil and sand high in the air and deafening the men with its roar. As the afterblast struck and debris rained down on them, two more shells exploded, even closer than the first, and Lampton, already obscured by the smoke, bawled, '*Let's go!*' He advanced on the run, away from the swirling smoke, and the men did the same.

It was clear, as they ran, that a fire fight had broken out ahead, where the SAF, Baluchi and *firqat* troops were spreading across the irregular, rocky terrain at the crouch, with mortar explosions erupting between them. Before Lampton's group reached that area, however, a Shpagin fired on them from the high ground, making them take cover behind some rocks. They returned the fire with their SLRs and M16s, but as such weapons were largely ineffective at such a range, the *adoo* machine-gun kept firing, turning the terrain around them into an inferno of boiling dust and flying debris, including hot gravel and pieces of barbed thorn bushes.

'Set up the mortar!' Lampton shouted at Bill as sand, dust and gravel showered them. 'Take that bastard out!'

The rest of the troop kept up a hail of return fire as Gumboot and Bill mounted the 7.62mm mortar on its steel baseplate. While they were doing so, Andrew ran up the lower slopes of the high ground, zigzagging from rock to rock, ignored by the machine-gun crew, still concentrating on the main group, though fired on by FN rifles from the same location. Eventually settling down behind some large boulders about halfway up the slope, south-west of the enemy position, he wrapped the GPMG sling around his body and waited for Bill and Gumboot to give him an opening.

From his position on high, Andrew was able to see both the enemy position on the high ground – revealed by the curling blue smoke from its roaring machine-gun – and the rest of his troop on the low ground, temporarily protected by a natural circle of rocks that was being devastated, and gradually torn apart, by the *adoo* machine-gunner.

Within the convulsion of sand and smoke created by the machine-gun fire, Bill and Gumboot had put the mortar together and were adjusting the alignment; Ricketts was giving covering fire with his SLR; and Sergeant Lampton was covering his left ear with one hand, blocking out the atrocious noise, while shouting into the radio mike.

Jock, though nominally in charge of the radio, was keeping watch with his M16 resting in the cradle of his left arm. Cocky as always, he waved at Andrew and then stuck his thumb up in the air.

An *adoo* sniper put a bullet through Jock's hand, making him scream and fall backwards, curling up and holding the wrist of his wounded hand with his free hand, amazed at the amount of blood pouring out.

Bill fired the mortar. The elevation was too low and the shell fell well behind the *adoo*'s machine-gun emplacement, though close enough to cover the gunners in a rain of soil and sand. As Bill and Gumboot increased the mortar's elevation, Ricketts kept up the covering fire with his SLR and Lampton took his first-aid kit out of his bergen and bandaged Jock's hand.

'It's bleeding a lot,' he said, wiping Jock's blood from his face, 'but the bullet went clean through and out the other side, so there's no lasting damage. You'll be in a lot of pain for a long time, but you won't be permanently damaged.'

'I'm fucking bleeding to death!' Jock responded, still holding his wrist and looking at the blood-stained bandage around his hand.

Lampton squeezed his shoulder. 'No, you're not. You're just bleeding a lot. It'll hurt and you'll have restricted mobility for a long time, but the hand will get better in due course. Now make sure that bandage stays tight – and keep in contact with the forward group through the radio. You can still work that, Jock.'

'OK, boss,' Jock said, then twitched when the mortar fired a second time. This time the shell fell even closer to the *adoo* sangar, but it still did not damage it. Jock rolled his eyes in mock despair. Lampton again squeezed his shoulder. 'You'll be OK,' he said, then turned away to do the leopard crawl up to Bill and Gumboot. 'You two couldn't hit a barn door,' he said, 'if the damned thing was stuck on your pricks. What the hell's going on?'

'We don't have a forward observer,' Bill said, 'so we can only guess the correct calibrations. But this time we'll get the cunts.'

'You will?'

'Yes, we will.'

'I depend on it,' Lampton said.

Ricketts was still blasting the hell out of the ground around the *adoo* sangar – not doing much damage, but keeping their heads down

– when Lampton crawled up to him and said, 'Good man. Keep it going.' Ricketts did not reply. He was too busy firing. Bill fired the mortar, making another awful racket, filling the vicinity with smoke, and the shell, which was clearly visible leaving the tube, arched over the hill at a very high elevation, then dropped down, like a bird shot in flight, on what seemed like the very heads of the *adoo*.

The explosion blew the stones of the sangar out a long way. When the smoke cleared, one dead body was clearly revealed, hanging over the remaining stones, his jellaba torn and bloody, with the bent and smouldering barrel of the machine-gun lying on top of him.

Some others, however, were clearly still alive and one of them stood up, screaming wildly, firing his Kalashnikov in a wide arc. Andrew stood up too, forgetting the rule book, supporting the GPMG with the sling around his body, holding the weapon in his right hand, the belt feed in his left, and spreading his legs to fire from the hip. The recoil pushed him back, but he leant forward, shaking visibly, and his sustained burst tore the remaining stones apart, exploding the sand and dust, then moved upwards to savage the *adoo* sniper and throw him back out of sight, his body riddled with bullets.

'Keep firing!' Lampton shouted and raced up

the hill, followed instantly by Ricketts, while Bill and Gumboot, forsaking the mortar, gave covering fire with their M16s.

Andrew kept firing, left and right, up and down, only stopping when Lampton and Ricketts almost reached the position. They raced into boiling dust, swirling smoke, the stench of cordite, and found Arabs slashed by shrapnel, scorched by the blast, peppered with bullets, pouring blood everywhere, with one of them still holding his *kunjias*, as if about to attack them. The bent barrel of the exploded machine-gun had crushed the skull of a gunner.

Lampton turned away and looked back down the hill, then he raised and lowered his right hand from shoulder level to hip, indicating, 'Follow me.'

'These diversions are holding us back,' he said to Ricketts. 'Let's catch up with the forward group.'

Without waiting for a reply, he waved to Andrew, still farther down the hill, then pointed forward with his forefinger. Understanding, Andrew waved back and started humping the GPMG onto his shoulders. Ricketts followed Lampton as he made his way obliquely down the hill, gradually falling back in front of the group on the rocky flatland that ran between the two sides of the wadi. Gumboot and Bill had broken the mortar down into its component parts and were now marching heavily burdened, holding their M16s at the ready. Bill looked less troubled now.

The fire fight was continuing where the forward group was located, with explosions from 81mm mortars and LAWS causing devastation. Though the sun was still sinking, painting the white rocks with gold, the troops were painfully advancing through an immense cloud of sand and dust. More accurately, they were moving left and right, between the eastern and western sides of the wadi, like men who did not quite know what to do. Though being devastated by *adoo* mortars and machine-guns, they still could not advance. Banked up behind them, spread across the flatland between the two sides of the wadi, were SAF and Baluchi soldiers, together with the SAS men who had advanced along the western side with their Land Rovers, Saladin armoured cars, and Omani suppliers with heavily laden donkeys. They had all stopped to find out what was happening.

'What the hell . . .?' As he often did, Lampton asked the question of no one in particular, then went off to look for an answer. In this case, he went no farther than another hundred yards, where, with Ricketts by his side and his other men behind him, he found Greenaway in heated consultation with Worthington and Parker.

'I'm sorry, boss,' Parker was saying, 'but they're adamant about this. They say it's the beginning of the religious festival of Ramadan, when they're forbidden to eat or drink between dawn and dusk. They're also forbidden to fight.'

'That's nonsense!' the CO replied, his face purple with rage. 'We know all about Ramadan, planned for it, discussed it, but because of the importance of this operation, the *firqats* were given a dispensation – not only by their religious leaders, but also by the Sultan himself. So they've no reason to lay down their arms.'

'Sorry, boss,' Parker replied, pointing to the mass of *firqats* who were leaving the assault force and heading back to the Ain watering-hole, 'but they aren't concerned with their religious leaders *or* the Sultan. Come what may, they're going to show proper respect for the religious festival of Ramadan. That means no eating, no drinking . . . and no fighting. They've already laid down their arms.'

'Damn it, Sergeant . . .!'

'Sorry, boss.'

'They can't desert us at this stage! We've already cleared most of the *adoo* off the plateau and driven them into the wadis around it. The

Sultan's forces can now control the area. If the *firqats* desert us at this point – just when we need to flush the remaining *adoo* out of the surrounding wadis – we'll have to abandon some of our positions and let the *adoo* come back in. If they do that, they'll mount a counter-attack.'

'They've just done it,' Worthington said, pointing towards the western hill.

Everyone looked automatically towards where he was pointing. They saw a vast, frightening number of *adoo* coming up over the rim of the western side of the wadi, all framed by a blood-red sun that appeared to be melting and dripping over them, painting the whole landscape in crimson. Even as the *adoo* marched down the hill, the dull thud of their firing mortars was heard.

'Damn!' Greenaway snapped.

The first shells exploded at the base of the western hill, throwing bodies into the air, shredding the flesh from some of the donkeys with flying red-hot shrapnel and obscuring those nearby in billowing sand and spiralling smoke. The bellowing of the donkeys did not drown the dreadful screams of the wounded men.

'We need the *firqats*,' Greenaway said.

'You won't get them,' Parker replied. 'Sorry, boss, they won't wear it.'

'I should have known,' Greenaway said.

'We live in hope,' Worthington told him. 'We either stand here and fight or make a tactical withdrawal and regroup where we have more support. What say you, boss?'

Greenaway looked at the western hill. The *adoo* were swarming down it. Their mortars were landing all along the base of the hill, killing animals and men, and clearing the way for an *adoo* advance back along the wadi, regaining what they had just lost. Greenaway scratched his nose, watched the mortar shells exploding, then turned to the radio operator beside Worthington. 'A tactical withdrawal,' he said, 'for the Western Group and its support teams, to regroup at the Ain watering-hole and wait for our instructions. The Eastern Group will . . .'

'Hold back those bastards,' Sergeant Parker interrupted, 'long enough for air support and for reinforcements to be transported in from Jibjat.'

'Yes, Sergeant,' Greenaway said. 'That sums it up nicely. RSM,' he said, turning to Worthington, 'get on that radio and do the necessary. Meanwhile, our Eastern Group will dig in here, out of range of the enemy mortars, and, if required, engage the enemy in hand-to-hand fighting. In short, we'll hold the hill as long as needs be. Any questions, gentlemen?'

'No, boss!' half a dozen voices sang out in unison.

'Good. Then let's do it.'

All along the line, while the *adoo* mortar explosions came closer and Major Greenaway was driven away to link up with the SAF, the radio operators communicated the CO's instructions to both action groups. Within minutes, the Western Group was making its withdrawal from the area being devastated by the *adoo* mortars – though some of the Saladin armoured cars, obviously given separate instructions, broke away from the retreating column and bounced across the rocky flatland to lend support to the Eastern Group.

'An encouraging sight,' Andrew murmured.

'We should turn those Saladins around,' Gumboot said, 'and send them after those fucking *firqats*. Blow the shit out of them'

'You can't dig in,' Lampton said, 'so I recommend sangars. The *adoo* will be here in half an hour, so don't hang around, lads.'

'With you all the way, boss,' Jock said. 'No need to say more.'

They all hurried to build their sangars, tearing the stones from the earth, but Gumboot, who was more scared than he looked, felt obliged to say something.

'Those dumb fucking *firqats*,' he said. 'I could shit on their couscous!'

Sergeant Parker walked up to him, grabbed

him by his webbing, tugged him forward until they were nose to nose, and said, 'Are you building a fucking sangar or aren't you?'

'Yes, boss, I am!'

'Then build it, Trooper. *Just build it*!'

Gumboot worked overtime – more scared of Parker than he was of the *adoo* – and the others, wanting no more aggravation, worked just as hard. They were encouraged in this not only by Parker's vehemence, but by the fact that the explosions from the *adoo* mortars were advancing from the base of the western hill to the SAS positions, even as the *adoo* troops – no longer impeded by the Western Group, which was now in tactical withdrawal – were advancing across the flatland and would soon be within the firing range of their AK-47 Kalashnikovs, FN rifles and RPD light machine-guns.

'Fuck!' groaned Gumboo. 'There's hundreds of them!'

'The man can count,' Andrew said.

They joked to quell the fear that even the hardiest felt when confronted with the possibility of death. Perhaps the jokes worked – at least they bought a breathing space – but when the *adoo* opened fire that primal fear was erased, leaving nothing but instinct and, as some thought, the lessons of Sickeners One and Two. By these they would now live or die.

'Fire at will!' Lampton bawled.

Gumboot and Bill had already set up their mortar and fired the first shell when Lampton shouted. Even before it had exploded in the midst of the advancing *adoo*, Andrew had opened up with his GPMG, and Ricketts and Lampton were firing their SLRs. Jock, who had the radio and could use it with one hand, was listening for incoming calls and wondering what he could do with his useless hand if the *adoo* overran them. He studied the bloody bandage around his hand and realized he was hurting.

'Shit!' Jock said as the first mortar shell fired by Bill exploded among the *adoo*. 'This is no fucking joke!'

Kneeling behind the wall, Ricketts fired his SLR, not knowing if he had hit anyone or not, only aware that he had to keep firing until he was stopped. He saw some of the enemy falling – shot by him or by someone else – and others blown apart in the explosions from the half-dozen SAS mortars in the sangars.

Almost deafened by a shocking roar, he glanced sideways and saw Andrew in the next sangar, standing upright, legs apart, firing the heavy GPMG from the hip and smiling in a distant, trancelike manner, unconcerned about dying.

'Get down, you stupid bastard!' Ricketts he screamed.

Andrew ignored him, being lost in his own world, seeing nothing but the hordes of *adoo* coming at him, skirting around mortar explosions, jerking epileptically in death, falling down and jumping up again to continue advancing.

Gumboot was with Bill, hurriedly reloading the mortar, fascinated by the sheer number of *adoo* coming at him and still unable to accept that the *firqats* had actually walked. He helped Bill adjust the elevation, then they fired another mortar round. Again, the shell exploded in the middle of the *adoo*, blowing some of them to hell, but those untouched emerged from the swirling smoke, still advancing determinedly. The pair were now loading and firing the mortar as quickly as possible. But the *adoo* kept advancing.

Like the others, Ricketts was convinced that his final hour had come, but he reloaded and fired with the expertise he had been given back in Hereford. Mortar shells were exploding around him, showering him with soil and sand, and gradually the thickening smoke obscured the advancing enemy. They were coming closer, however, firing on the march, making the sand spit viciously around the sangars, and sending bullets ricocheting noisily off the stones. An SAS trooper screamed, jerking backwards and collapsing. A whole sangar took a direct mortar hit and was blown to hell, with its troopers slashed by shrapnel and crushed by stones, their bodies covered in dust.

Ricketts fired his SLR. He saw the *adoo* drawing nearer. He thought of Maggie back home – it was just a flash of her lovely face – then he unholstered his Browning handgun and laid it down on the wall. He could hear the excited shouts of the *adoo*; which meant they were now very close. He saw the first of them emerging from the smoke, so he fired a sustained blast. They spasmed and collapsed. Others took their place. Some were firing Kalashnikovs or FN rifles, but others were waving their *kunjias*, prepared for hand-to-hand fighting.

Ricketts felt a bolt of fear. It shot through him, passing on. When it had gone, he experienced a great peace and heightened awareness. He fired his SLR until it was empty, then dropped it and picked up the Browning and climbed to his feet. The men around him were throwing grenades, which exploded and were followed by screaming. Jock was firing his Browning handgun with his good hand and Sergeant Lampton, standing beside him, was ducking to avoid the gleaming blade of a swinging *kunjias*.

Ricketts took aim with his Browning, holding it two-handed. He waited until he saw the whites of the *adoo*'s eyes above his *shemagh*, then he fired a double-tap and swung towards another man even before his first victim had fallen.

Before he reached his thirteenth shot, the ground around him roared and erupted, picking him up and slamming him back down into a whirlpool of light and pain. He passed out and regained consciousness, choking, spitting sand, then rolled painfully onto his back and looked directly above him.

An *adoo* with a *shemagh* across his mouth was standing above Ricketts, legs apart, holding a *kunjias* on high, about to split Ricketts in two with it.

Ricketts turned his head aside, not wanting to face the knife, and saw Gumboot rolling out of a subsiding cloud of dust as Bill ran forward, firing his Browning at the *adoo* standing over Ricketts. The Arab screamed and staggered back, dropping his *kunjias*. The long blade fell dangerously close to Ricketts's head as the Arab fell and the ground erupted under Bill.

Ricketts saw Bill picked up, flipped over and slammed down, screaming in an indescribable manner, with his lower half missing. Ricketts had to look away, but then he saw one of Bill's legs, severed at the hip and pumping blood from the mangled, scorched stump. Ricketts looked back and saw Bill's staring, dazed eyes. His arms and upper half were shaking in a spasm as the blood poured out of his legless torso to drain him completely.

As Bill died, his gaze freezing, Gumboot climbed to his feet. He withdrew his Fairburn-Sykes knife from his belt and launched himself at the *adoo* running at him with his raised *kunjias*. They collided and were lost in the general mêlée as the roaring of the Strikemasters and Skyvans came down from the sky.

Ricketts was in great pain, and passed out again. He recovered a few minutes later, brought back to painful consciousness by the fire in his left leg. Gritting his teeth to stop his groaning, he saw the men still fighting around him, most of them locked in mortal hand-to-hand combat, most screaming or shouting. Looking beyond them, through the dense, swirling smoke, he saw the Strikemasters diving on the high ground of the western hill with their guns roaring relentlessly. Even as they did so, one of the Skyvans came into view, flying low across the flat plain, its crew rolling out a series of Burmail bombs which exploded in the midst of the *adoo* still advancing, engulfing them in a vast wall of yellow flames.

Ricketts groaned again and tried to crawl out of his sangar, the walls of which had been badly damaged and scorched by a mortar blast. Even as he saw the reinforcements arriving in Bedfords, Land Rovers and Saladin armoured cars, all firing on the move, he was seized by another spasm of pain and passed out again. He drifted down a tunnel of darkness that took him to Maggie's face. There he found solace.

18

Ricketts recovered consciousness in Sergeant Whistler's Skyvan, which was flying the wounded and a lot of the dead back to RAF Salalah. The dead, mostly *adoo*, had been placed in body bags and just heaped on the aircraft floor, one on top of the other, then lashed down with web straps. Already, only halfway back to Salalah, the combined weight of the bodies was squeezing out body fluids and blood, creating what would soon become a foul smell.

When Ricketts had recovered enough to discuss the grisly scene around him, he was informed by Whistler that each time the Skyvans arrived at RAF Salalah, where the bodies were removed, the cargo compartment had to be hosed down by an RAF fire-engine. The SAF dead, he said, would be taken away for military burial. The *adoo* dead would be put on public display in the main square of Salalah as a demonstration to the locals that the Sultan's Armed Forces were winning the war.

Transferred from the Skyvan to the hospital in RAF Salalah, Ricketts learnt that his leg had been impregnated with many pieces of shrapnel, but that no lasting damage had been done. His mobility would be unimpaired once the wounds had healed. He also learnt that the *adoo* counter-attack in the Wadi Dharbat had been defeated with the arrival of the air support and reinforcements from Jibjat.

While resting up in hospital, waiting to be flown back to Hereford, he was visited by Sergeant Lampton and Gumboot, who informed him that Jock and Andrew had already been flown home, the former to have his wounded hand attended to, the latter to receive treatment for a minor wound in his left arm, received in hand-to-hand fighting with an *adoo* wielding a *kunjias*.

'Andrew won the fight,' Gumboot said, 'and he didn't stop crowing about it until he was flown back to Hereford.'

Ricketts was flown back on 3 October, just as the most dangerous phase of the operation in Oman was beginning. By that time B Squadron and G Squadron 22 SAS, the Firqat Khalid bin Waalid, and one company of the SAF had advanced some fifteen miles into communist-held territory and built three defensive positions on the sun-scorched Jebel Khaftawt. This became known as the Leopard Line. From there, the SAF moved out to dominate the surrounding area with an intensive 'aggressive-patrol' programme designed to clear the remaining *adoo* out of their lime caves and sangars in the wadis.

For ten days the SAS fought a running battle around the high plain, with SAF Skyvan tactical transporters, flown by British pilots, flying in supplies and ammunition, and SAS teams guiding Omani Strikemasters in strafing attacks on the *adoo* positions.

Again, the *firqats* threatened to stop fighting. This time they were insisting that their donkeys and camels be taken off the Jebel and transported to market. When this was done, with SAF jet fighters acting as escorts for the livestock, the *firqats* returned to the fray.

Eventually Operation Jaguar established the Sultan's Armed Forces on the Jebel Dhofar, which was seen as a significant defeat for the *adoo*. This success was crowned when the *adoo*, determined to rectify their great loss, launched and lost the legendary battle for Mirbat, which took place approximately nine months after Operation Jaguar, in July 1972.

Ricketts, Jock and Andrew had recovered from their wounds and were told about Mirbat when they were having drinks with Sergeant Lampton and Gumboot in the Paludrine Club at the SAS base in Hereford.

On 18 July a group of *adoo* deliberately allowed themselves to be seen by SAF forces in order to lure away the 60 *firqats* supporting the nine-man BATT team in Mirbat. This left only 30 *Askars* holding the Wali Fort and 25 gendarmes in the Dhofar Gendarmerie fort, located 900 yards north of the northern perimeter.

With the *firqats* gone, 250 of the *adoo*'s best warriors marched on Mirbat, armed with Kalashnikov AK-47s, light, heavy and medium machine-guns, two 75mm recoilless anti-tank rifles, an 84mm Carl Gustav rocket launcher, and mortars of various calibres, up to 82mm. Arriving at Mirbat, the *adoo* broke up into numerous combat groups and encircled the town. At 0530, the *adoo* attacked the DG fort, killing four of the gendarmes, but losing the element of surprise.

Once the fire fight had commenced, the guerrillas in the hills rained mortar bombs on the DG fort, the BATT house, and the town itself. On the roof of the BATT house, SAS corporals Peter Wignall and Roger Chapman were firing the settlement's only GPMG and an 0.5in Browning heavy machine-gun. With them on the roof was their 23-year-old commander, Captain Mike Kealy. Below them, in a pit at the base of the building, Lance-Corporal Harris was operating an 81mm mortar. In the gun-pit next to the DG fort, the enormous Fijian, Corporal Labalaba, was firing the 25-pounder with the aid of an Omani gunner, Walid Khamis. A second Fijian, Trooper Savesaki, was manning the gun-pit's short-range radio.

With the *adoo* swarming in on the town and settlement from all sides, Captain Kealy drafted an urgent request for reinforcements to provisional HQ at Salalah. As he was doing so, the *adoo* were firing on the DG fort and the settlement with Soviet RPG-7 rockets and their Carl Gustav 84mm rocket launcher. At approximately 0700 hours, Savesaki informed Captain Kealy by short-range radio that Labalaba had been badly wounded in the chin. Hearing this, Kealy called immediately for a helicopter to attempt a casevac.

While Lance-Corporal Chapman bravely ran from the BATT house, through the shell-torn town, to mark a helicopter landing zone near the beach for the casevac, Captain Kealy and a medical orderly, Trooper Tobin, crossed 400 yards of open ground, under enemy fire, to attend to the wounded Fijian. They found the Omani gunner, Walid Khamis, lying on his back, seriously wounded. Labalaba, though wearing a shell dressing on his face to staunch the flow of blood from his terrible chin wound, was still loading and firing the big gun, unaided. Savesaki, though bleeding from serious head and shoulder wounds, was propped up against the wall of the bunker and continuing to fire his rifle at the approaching *adoo*. One dead gendarme was lying in the gun-pit; another was on the parapet of the DG fort, sprawled across his machine-gun.

While the medical orderly attended to the wounded, Kealy sent a short-range radio message back to the BATT house, telling them to call for an air strike.

Shortly after, Labalaba was shot dead and Tobin had his jaw shot away. The latter was then also wounded badly in the back and hand by an *adoo* fragmentation grenade.

Meanwhile, on the beach, Chapman had thrown a green smoke grenade to mark the landing zone for the casevac helicopter. However, as the chopper approached the LZ, the *adoo*, now strongly reinforced and more heavily armed, fired on it from dead ground near the DG fort. Chapman therefore threw a red smoke grenade, warning off the helicopter. He dived for cover as the chopper flew away, its cabin peppered with machine-gun bullets, but luckily not damaged otherwise.

By now, the *adoo* were only thirty yards from

the gun-pit and adjoining ammunition bunker, hammering both positions, as well as the DG fort, with their rocket launcher, a hail of hand-grenades and a fusillade of small-arms fire.

The wounded Savesaki continued firing back, as did Captain Kealy, who was lightly grazed on the head by a bullet.

Just as the first of the *adoo* were about to overrun the gun-pit, two SAF Strikemasters, guided in by Kealy, now on the radio in the ammunition bunker, flew over the settlement, just above ground level, to attack the guerrillas with 7.62mm machine-guns and 500-lb bombs. Kealy was alternating his target guidance for the Strikemasters with instructions to his mortar team in the BATT house, 400 yards away.

In the BATT house's mortar pit, Lance-Corporal Harris found that the *adoo* were so close that he could not elevate the barrel high enough. He solved the problem by lifting the heavy steel tripod off the ground, pulling the burning-hot barrel against his chest, gripping the rest of the weapon between his legs and dropping the bombs down the barrel by hand. As Harris was doing this, Corporal Bob Bradshaw, in the BATT house, was directing the second wave of Strikemasters by radio.

The aircraft hammered the *adoo* machine-guns overlooking the town, then made several attacks on the guerrillas on the dead ground near the fort on the northern perimeter. One of the Strikemasters was damaged by machine-gun fire and had to return to Salalah.

At 0915, when Captain Kealy was giving water to the wounded and re-dressing their injuries, G Squadron 22 SAS flew by chopper, almost at sea level, from Salalah to the Mirbat beach, landing during the second Strikemaster attack on the hundreds of *adoo* massed around the northern perimeter.

Eighteen men from G Squadron marched inland in two groups to wipe out a position held by five guerrillas. A second group of SAS men, advancing south from the beach and operating in three-man teams, engaged in successful fire fights with three *adoo* positions.

Other guerrillas surrendered to SAS troopers guarding the helicopter LZ by the beach. By 1030, the wounded, including the Omani gunner, Walid Khamis, the Fijian trooper Savesaki, and the unfortunate medical orderly, Trooper Tobin, were casevacked by helicopter, though Tobin later died of his terrible wounds.

The retreating *adoo* lost at least forty men – perhaps thirty dead, and ten wounded and taken prisoner – as well as the last of their prestige. The battle begun with Operation Jaguar was completed with the Battle for

Mirbat, which became a turning-point in the war, ultimately leading to defeat for the *adoo*.

The 'secret' war in Oman remained secret for many years, but that night in July 1972, in the Paludrine Club, the survivors of the campaign, including Ricketts, Gumboot, Jock, Andrew and Sergeant Lampton, were able to toast their lost friends with a great deal of pride.

They did not discuss the dead, or those who had failed to 'beat the clock', but engaged in their traditional, good-natured bullshit before making their way back to their bashas.

'Where are we going next?' Gumboot asked as they entered the dark, silent spider.

'Belfast,' Lampton replied briskly. 'Have pleasant dreams, lads.'

The men groaned melodramatically, then crept off to the spider, and their beds.